M000283682

CHURCH AT THE
WALL

Stories of Hope along the San Diego-Tijuana Border

SETH DAVID CLARK

JUDSON PRESS
PUBLISHERS SINCE 1824
VALLEY FORGE, PA

Library of Congress Cataloging-in-Publication data

Names: Clark, Seth (Seth David), author.
Title: Church at the wall : stories of hope along the San Diego-Tijuana
   border / Seth David Clark.
Description: Valley Forge, PA : Judson Press, 2022. | Includes
   bibliographical references.
Identifiers: LCCN 2021038117 (print) | LCCN 2021038118 (ebook) | ISBN
   9780817018306 (paperback) | ISBN 9780817082345 (epub)
Subjects: LCSH: Border Church (San Diego-Tijuana)
Classification: LCC BX9999.S28 C53 2022 (print) | LCC BX9999.S28 (ebook)
   | DDC 280.0972/23--dc23
LC record available at https://lccn.loc.gov/2021038117
LC ebook record available at https://lccn.loc.gov/2021038118

Printed in the U.S.A.

First printing, 2022.

CONTENTS

ACKNOWLEDGMENTS

I owe a debt of gratitude to many people—all of whom have made possible these words in straightforward and circuitous ways. These include, but are not limited to: Lisa Blair, Nancy Clark, Mark Douglas, John Fanestil, Maria Teresa Fernandez, Tuli Ghosh, Susanne Johnson, Karla, Paul John Martin, Tania Mendoza, Guillermo Navarrete, Cheryl Price, Christian Ramirez, Robert Vivar, Daniel Watman, and all those who participated in the Seth Wants to Write a Book Club. It may go without saying, but I owe a debt of thanks to my family, especially my wife. Championing my involvement in multiple ministries while going through a doctoral program—and then writing a book!—takes a sturdy and selfless spirit that few spouses have. Verna does. *Mil gracias, mi amor. Siempre te quiero.*

INTRODUCTION:

A TYPICAL SUNDAY CHURCH

I was heading to that wall again. It just happened to be the first time I had been to the Border Church since the rains dried up one year before the pandemic changed our practice to something radically different from what it had been for years. Regardless, at that moment, my destination lay within an operational zone of the United States Customs and Border Protection: a park amid migrant patrols and military-style maneuvers. More importantly, beyond two giant fences and the technological moat in between, were my friends. These friends were not simply amigos I would meet at the aptly named International Friendship Park; they were also my coreligionists. On that day, we assembled to worship the God of all things.

Here, at the meeting place of two nations and the world's largest ocean, we gathered atop Monument Mesa under the shadow of two towers. One, El Faro (the lighthouse), sits perched above Playa de Tijuana, Mexico's northwesternmost neighborhood. The other is a high-tech US watchtower, standing tall over the Imperial Beach—the most low-key of the San Diego area's beach cities. One tower warns sailors of the sea's edge; the other informs agents of impositions on sovereign might. Both towers promote a version of safety. I'll admit I prefer the former.

Although this trip was my first of the dry season, I had hardly forsaken seeing *mis* amigxs y hermanxs. Only the flooded road was different, not my companionship with these friends and siblings in Christ. During the wet season, which I confess isn't wet by much of the world's standards, the Tijuana River Valley floods. Its namesake river flows mostly westward and ever so slightly northward from the heart of Tijuana, across the international boundary, and out to the Pacific Ocean. As the waters travel through the canyonlands of northern Baja, they carry garbage, feces, and a plethora of leftover automotive liquids with them. The reeking, noxious brew bubbles under the fence, through some frequently failing treatment measures, and right over the single road to the park—the one I must traverse.

When the sludge has dried, a car can drive through the river valley, following a road from the exterior parking lot of Border Field State Park to a parking lot on Monument Mesa, in about four minutes. During the wet season, the road is only passable by foot; the route takes upwards of forty minutes, even if we're not ambling. When the road is so wet that even boots aren't enough to keep the contaminants off one's skin, we travel the detour—a horse trail—taking us out to the beach and down the oceanfront sands. All that detouring can take an hour.

Breaking away from my other commitments as pastor of the First Baptist Church of National City puts the squeeze on my Sunday. Most pilgrimages are methodical and meditative. This one is hurried when wet. I imagine, for on-site US clergy who do not have the same Sunday morning church duties, the pedestrian journey to Border Church is more reflective and prayerful than mine. The path of prayerful pilgrimage is so winsome for some that, even when the road opens up to cars for the summer, some clergy continue making the pilgrimage on foot when they can.

On that summer Sunday in 2019, I found the road open. I proceeded to drive my car through the state park for the first time in months. Unhurried, I was more open to my surroundings, and with that openness came a sadness, a dark moment of realization.

At the point where the road turns south, I was taken aback by a ghastly sight. In front of me stood a newly erected secondary border fence. My eyes were fixed on the shrapnel jutting intentionally out of the wounded earth. It cut to the quick.

This spectacle is simply one snapshot of sadness, grief, and anger amid countless other emotions along the borderlands. Yet, this book does not linger on the sadness of fences and fissions. Nor is it a call to stick our heads in the sand to continue in a state of happy ignorance. My aim is to provide an authentic and accurate look at the realities of the border and the Border Church. Here, hurt and happiness exist together, where they invade each other's boundaries.

We cannot disregard the evils on display at the border. Nevertheless, I want to focus on the light instead of the darkness, pure things rather than vulgar displays of power, and the now-and-forever reign of the Divine over the transient empires of geopolitics. To know the former items truly, we cannot disregard the latter, but the direction of our focus matters. Like the liminal in-between state of the Border Church itself, this book sits in a liminal space between ever-present grief and pervasive hope, as the reader will see in the stories and theology in its pages.

First, let's consider the Border Church in a little more detail.

Regardless of how they get there, the pastors and visitors to the US side of the Border Church must arrive at Friendship Park, half of which sits within a border-enforcement zone on the US side. As such, visiting civilians entering the tiny, "friendly" area can only come into what the Border

Patrol calls "Friendship Circle" at the discretion of Border Patrol officers.

Here, a gate opens to the public for four hours each Saturday and four hours again on Sunday. At the entrance, a posted sign reads: "10 persons only." It used to say "25," but the Border Patrol changed it at their sole discretion. ("Discretion" seems to be one of their favorite words.) Even the ten-person rule is at the discretion of the public relations agent staffing the area during open hours. If the pastor arrives with three visitors while nine people are inside communicating with family and friends through the thick mesh of the border, the agent can, in theory, let four more people inside the park. However, the sad history of the practice is that more and more pressure on these agents from their superiors leads to less and less flexibility with the ten-person rule. Granted, agents sometimes allow the clergyperson along with ten visitors, but churchgoers and families rarely receive the same leniency.

This dynamic routinely puts us in the awkward position of being asked to choose to bring in our church attendees at the expense of the families present, having access to their loved ones. We would never agree to family removal and separation for our sake; part of our *raison d'etre* is to support these very families, whether or not we know them.

Thus, a chat commences. I have seen negotiations about numbers happen between and among various people: the agent and the minister, the minister and the visitors, and sometimes even the visitors and the agent. It is not easy, but it is worth it. I ponder how this lack of power to accomplish their vision would give church-growth "saviors" a heart attack.

Once inside our worship space, the US pastor approaches the wall. On the other side, the faithful have already set up canopies and a sound system; they begin cooking a pot of something with an aroma as tantalizing as it is forbidden in its acquisition. Ministering within their community, they are engaging in fellowship that is both worlds apart and inches away from my colleagues and me.

Since we cannot see or hear far beyond the wall, we often have to shout through its rusting metal. Or if the notoriously spotty cell phone reception of the borderlands allows, we can send a message that we have arrived. Further negotiations commence through the mesh of the border fence, where we discuss the church's business at our single church wall. The leaders finalize the order of service, connect the wireless microphone in the US to the sound system in Mexico, and troubleshoot any other logistical issues—the secular "sacraments" anticipating the spiritual sacrament that is soon to come.

While there's an actual table for the sacramental elements in Tijuana, to the north by mere inches is a cloth mat with a wooden chalice, dyed purple after all these years, and a plain wooden plate to carry grape juice and bread to the faithful. Images of communion celebration are enlarged and placed between the worshippers and the fence to visually take us back to—and provide historical hope for—a time when communion practice through the wall included only one loaf and one cup.

Around 1:30, after the final preparation concludes, we worship. Sometimes glitches or latecomers delay the start, but eventually we worship. Beginning worship as close to 1:30 as possible is crucial to those on the US side because, at 2:00, we have to be out of the border enforcement zone whether or not the service is over. Something as simple as time highlights the stark cultural difference between US seminary-graduated pastors and a grassroots group of *Tijuanenses*, deportees, and migrants. The US federal government's long arm certainly has a wrist watch of its own and adds to the cultural conflict. Regardless, church starts around 1:30 and ends promptly at 2:00 for those on the US side; on the Mexico side, church ends whenever it is finished. Our binational, bilingual communion service opens with an announcement of who we are as a church at the wall and a welcome to an open table. Every week, all in attendance hear the following declaration in two languages: "It does not matter if you are a part of this church or any church. You are welcome here, and you are welcome to participate with us as much as you feel comfortable." This welcoming spirit invites people into the music, the prayers and prayer requests, the reading of scripture, and—most importantly—the communion table.

The Border Church's liturgy or order of service is similar to many other churches and traditions rooted in Protestantism. I hope the following stories will call attention to what stands out to those who can be there: a weekly practice of binational communion in which all are welcome. The practice of communion stands out because this is an act of unity. A physically exemplified union serves as a critical prophetic call amid political division. In no small part, its call reverberates strongly as an act of "withness" and collaboration following the history of Christianity that has, again and again, proved rife with division. With that reality all too obvious in the historical background and a current material barrier between the US congregants and those in Mexico, we stand to counteract division and seek to remove barriers between all persons.

Traveling from Tijuana to the wall is undoubtedly different from traveling in the US. Tijuana's vehicles carry not only people but also stuff—lots of stuff. All of the equipment is stored in a trailer at a local resident's home to be picked up mid-morning and towed on the day of worship by Guillermo Navarrete, the lay pastor in charge of the Border Church's Mexico side.

Our Mexican sisters and brothers meet at the western-most border monument, under the lighthouse that gives the church one of its colloquial names, El Faro. It is from this very lighthouse that the church powers its electrical devices. Unique agreements, most of which I doubt exist in writing, ensure that the church can operate without impairment or harassment from local businesses or officials. As Jesus said, it pays to make deals with people in high places. At the very least, he said something like that.

With the external and internal infrastructure on-site, volunteers arrive in the late morning to set everything up. The meal of the day gets prepared or comes ready for distribution, packed inside disposable dinnerware. (Packing in and packing out may be a mainstay of wilderness ventures, but it also rings true here in one of the busiest cities in Mexico.) After the setup ends, so begins the church's interpersonal ministry. Mexican citizens in Tijuana make up the core of the Border Church, but the lion's share of the attendees are migrants hoping to journey into the US and deportees whose US sojourns have been cut short.

The prior week's work in shelters elicits the attendance of expectant US immigrants. Sometimes, migrants temporarily live near the fence and don't need more than a verbal invite shortly before the service. Canyons cover this particular border terrain, and some live there as well. Still others who come are newly deported persons striving to find peace amidst disorientation as well as more well-settled deportees who see this place of friendship and its congregation as a beacon of hope as powerful as its namesake lighthouse. Lunch is offered after the invitation to worship and is provided regardless of people's choice to worship with us. Regulars know when the service is over; they come a little closer when it is time to eat. Sometimes, they can even get a new toothbrush or blanket.

Besides the many Spanish speakers, often we have guests—Anglophonic visitors from North American churches, colleges, and nonprofits—who want to experience the border and its worship life. Diversity is never a surprise within this parish.

Once the worship service begins, both sides' voices are readily heard along and across the dividing line. A Mexican may give the welcome and opening prayer. The skilled Mexican music leader, Jaime Luis, who has been doing this since he was only a teenager, will invariably lead some modern worship songs. A visiting guest to Tijuana may read the Bible passage in English and a regular attendee read it in Spanish. Un estadounidense (a US citizen) and pastor will likely give the sermon of the day—more of a devotional thought that spans all of five or six minutes tops after translation. The prayer of confession, offer of pardon, and call to pass a sign of peace may come from either side. The symbol of peace is a pinky kiss through the mesh of the barrier wall—the pinky tip is all that fits there. The corresponding "Peace of Christ" and "*Paz de Cristo*" travel as sound waves through that same mesh.

The Border Patrol put a hard stop to sharing one loaf and one cup binationally years ago out of the felt need to enforce more vigilance. Now, congregants must partake of Holy Communion remembering the person and the work of Jesus anew, using two separate sets of elements. Though we can never physically share that meal, the nature of sound allows us to share in a benediction and announcements, time permitting. More often than not, the day's on-site US minister gives a blessing while packing up the church's diminutive American setup into the mobile supply backpack. On occasion, I have given a benediction while slowly walking backward out of the federal law enforcement zone where I do church.

After concluding the service, those in Mexico share the meal with one another and, in a symbolic way, turn the communion table into a table of fellowship. We talk about tables a lot at the Border Church, which is funny considering that the Border Patrol does not allow tables (or chairs, even for the elderly) inside their operations zone. One spiritual theme we proclaim is turning the border wall itself into the table of the Lord. I like that, but I'd like it more if we could literally turn the fence on its side so that we could share in the Lord's Supper and the lunchtime fellowship meal atop it. Sadly, lunch offers no physical nor social support to those in the US making the pilgrimage back to our cars, often through a river of sewage. Yet, as the church gathers for lunch in a sensible-yet-still-spiritual communion, there is a true and tangible benefit for many, particularly those who have been displaced and may not know where their next meal will come from.

On the US side, I get to know the visitors to the Border Church or the families coming to Friendship Park as I walk back to my car. Not infrequently, especially during the colder, wetter months, I walk in solitude. In those times, I review the experience in my mind, talk to God, enjoy the natural beauty around me, and find that I'm longing for connection with my friends and their food. Even then, I prefer the pace of this portion of the pilgrimage to the hurried uncertainty of heading toward the wall.

My fellow US clergy and I get to go home after the service, but not all who attend the Border Church have a home nearby. Some attendees, particularly asylum seekers from Honduras, El Salvador, and Guatemala—what was dubbed Golden Triangle by the CIA in an earlier epoch of US-Latin American relations—would be murdered if they returned to their home countries. Many sought but were denied asylum in my home country. Some have died upon returning home after not being found credible enough by my nation's law enforcers, and justice imparters refused to believe their lived realities.

We do not count "butts in the seats" at the Border Church or take down names for records to give to the next generation. The ethereal nature of the congregation has a certain attraction. More than that, the hands of unjust officials are powerful—and intruding. Without record-keeping, there is little way of knowing whether asylum seekers who once ate communion or lunch with us went on to greener pastures or went home to their deaths. Given that thousands of travelers have taken part in the ministry of the Border Church, it is not at all unlikely that some who have worshiped with us were murdered after deportation.

A similarly deadly fate waits for many of the deportees so disoriented that they can't stand to stay in Mexico. They consider the US their home yet fail to make it there through the remote Otay Mountains east of San Diego or more secluded and vast desert lands beyond them. Thousands of migrants—people made in the image and likeness of God— have died in the US wilderness seeking a life of promise. I do not know how many of these lost ones have graced our path at the Border Church, but I'm grateful that, at the very least, we were there, at the wall, every week, to offer them a bit of their daily bread when they came.

Many migrant journeys, both good and bad, will never be known to me, but those I know, I cherish deeply. I am so glad that this book passes on to you a few stories, my dear reader. These historical snapshots, though undoubtedly unfit for any world of happy make-believe, are filled with hope from and for the real world. I see that hope rooted in the reign of God; it's one that I await expectantly and one that I see glimpses of right here in the borderlands.

ABOUT THIS BOOK

This book is written about the Border Church, but it is not an all-encompassing description of that community of practice. Try as we might, nothing can fully be known on this terrestrial plane; an organization is an organism that goes beyond complete description. The physics of quantum theory has taught me, as a humanities person, that even the observation of some object alters the object itself. We are interacting with a universe of subjects here, as well, as I highlight a handful of true stories from the Border Church community. Each tale displays a theological value or practice of the Border Church in action. Beyond the snapshots themselves, I have also weaved theological discussion into every chapter so that the reader can find some new or retold truth about God. With this, I hope to offer practical considerations for one's own context. Whether or not, my dear reader, you find agreement in the theology I propose, I hope it stirs within you a fervor for God and encourages you to build a place-based practice of your own that stands present with and for marginalized persons and peoples.

Each chapter in this book pairs a borderlands story with a truth pursued and valued by the Border Church. All of the people portrayed in the subsequent pages are real. Each one has had an impact on and has been impacted by the worship of the Border Church at the border wall. Chapter one contains the story of John Fanestil, the founder of the Border Church, as a subject within God's *basileia* (the Greek word for "kingdom" or "reign"). Chapter two picks up the theme of faith and faithfulness through the lens of Maria Teresa Fernandez, the photo documentarian of Friendship Park and the Border Church. Chapter three pairs the theological concept of hope with the story of Karla, an asylum seeker failed by the US but not by God. Chapter four takes up Tania Mendoza's story as a deported mother separated from her only daughter, view through the lens of love. Chapter five takes a trip with Guillermo Navarrete, the lay pastor and unofficial tour guide of the Mexican side of Border Church, within the theological vehicle of accompaniment. Chapter six considers Dan Watman, a borderlands and immigrant rights activist and friend of the Border Church, through the theological concept of friendship. Chapter seven departs from narratives to a sojourn of free-verse poetry, explaining my transformation from theory to praxis, moving beyond solely being woke to taking action. Chapter eight is about Robert Vivar, a church leader on the Mexican side and deported immigrant rights advocate who specializes in the rights of deported veterans, and his battle for peace. The book wraps up with a brief epilogue.

I include myself as a subject in this book; this book comes from my vantage point. As such, I feel it is appropriate to tell you a little more about myself.

I prefer simply to be called by my given name: Seth. I identify as a middle-class white Protestant cisgender heterosexual male US citizen. I am married to a lovely woman named Verna. Before meeting her in college, I grew up in the Midwest. Since meeting Verna—may her forbearance be praised!—I have earned four degrees, including a doctorate of ministry. I, alongside Verna, parent two young children: Maximus Vincentius and Anastasia Sofia Luz. The life I've led so far has given me a perspective unlike that of anyone else in the Border Church community. Despite these differences, we share in a common humanity filled with hurts and hopes.

What I have accomplished and continue to do is not merely the result of my personal effort. I have the requisite training to think theologically and critically about Christian practices and the cultural environs. Some would call this privilege; I realize others may give my status different descriptors. Whatever the descriptor, it must acknowledge that I have benefitted from systems that were and are not readily available to the vast majority of those who find solace in the Border Church.

TO SEEK THE *BASILEIA* OF GOD

The *Basileia* of God

Having grown up in a tradition that appreciated the memorization of Bible verses, I can still recall Matthew 6:33—in the King James Version, of course—pretty well without having to look it up. "But seek ye first the kingdom [βασιλεία, *basileia*] of God, and his righteousness; and all these things shall be added unto you" (Matthew 6:33, KJV).

But did I know its theology in those days of my youth? Not entirely. And, at this point, I would argue that the meaning of the whole of the Word is more important than any given word. So what is this "kingdom" or *basileia* that Jesus talks about?

The *basileia* of God is the foundation of the good news that Jesus has to offer. In the above verse, the thrust of a disciple's life is clear: Seek the *basileia*, a feminine noun in Greek that translates to "kingdom," "realm," and "reign." Some also call it the "kin-dom." [1] No matter what it's called, to follow Christ's way, a disciple must seek it above all else. This life is not about seeking food, drink, or clothing. God wants to give those things to each of us, but they are secondary. First and foremost, God wants us to seek the divine *basileia*.

Further along in the story of this first Gospel of ours, one disciple uses violence, rather than Christ's peace, to obtain this *basileia* of heaven. His use of the sword receives no Messianic praise, but a rebuke from the King (Matthew 26:51-52). In the fourth Gospel, the frequently overzealous Peter effectively makes use of violence as he cuts off the ear of Malchus, a servant of the presiding High Priest (John 18:10-11). In the third Gospel, the whole act ends not only in rebuke but also in the last recorded miracle of Jesus' pre-crucifixion ministry—the healing of an enemy (Luke 22:50-51). With these and other *basileia* tenets in mind, ones that are so upside down from the world's use of power and dominion, I do not and cannot advocate for a here-and-now Christian theocracy resulting from or in force or dominion theology.

Instead of religious violence, Jesus responded to human powers in this world with nonviolence. Christ's kingship is displayed in the nonviolence of taking up the cross—for Jesus and for his followers. Like several contemporary biblical and theological scholars, I see this *basileia* of God as the crux of the matter for Jesus. I generally agree with Australian Michael Bird's definition of the good news of Jesus: "The gospel is the announcement that God's *basileia* has come in the life, death, and resurrection of Jesus of Nazareth, the Lord and Messiah, in fulfillment of Israel's Scriptures. The gospel evokes faith, repentance, and discipleship; its accompanying effects include salvation and the gift of the Holy Spirit."[2]

In other words, Christ's good news is that the *basileia* of God comes in the person and work of Jesus of Nazareth. Divine rulership does not come from our violence. Instead, our violence against the Divine One was flipped on its head when Jesus miraculously moved from death to life. That we can and will be saved is not the good news itself; the good news is that the *basileia* has come. Yet, salvation is not separate from the good news. In fact, it is one of the primary fruits of the very *basileia* which makes the gospel good. Seeking the *basileia* of God is seeking the heart of what the good news is all about.

After the *basileia*, the second thing that Jesus commands in the Bible verse above is to seek God's righteousness. Growing up, I had no idea that the original language said to seek God's δικαιοσύνη (*dikaiosunē*). The older definition of uprightness or being in a right relationship with others (especially God) is lost on most of our contemporaries. Aside from sermons and surfers, the only time a modern-day person utters "righteous" is when they lament self-righteous people and systems—hardly the righteous thrust of what Jesus was commanding.

I am all about big theological words, but as a general rule, I don't believe in the use of insider jargon to describe the fundamentals of our faith. Fortunately, *dikaiosunē* has another entirely accurate and relatively understandable translation: justice.

Jesus commands us to seek God's *basileia* and God's justice. We find it in Christ, but let me inform you, just in case you haven't made it that far into the New Testament, that Jesus ascended back up into the sky. So, can we seek God's *basileia* and justice in the here and now?

Praise God we can! But how?

Biblical theologian Nicholas Perrin describes living a *basileia* life now with a bit of musicality. He says:

> Life in the kingdom [basileia] *is something like jazz. With jazz, everyone knows it when they hear it; the problem is, no one can really define it. It's a little like that when it comes to following Jesus in his kingdom* [basileia]. *We know kingdom* [basileia] *discipleship when we see it, but initiating the*

process or thinking it through can be difficult, especially if we don't know how to define it.[3]

Thankfully, jazz—and the signs of the *basileia* of God in place in the present day—can be described truthfully, though incompletely, if we simply learn how to do so.

Perrin goes on to indicate that one of the signs of the presence of God's *basileia* in the here-and-now is that the good news is preached to "the poor." Perrin argues that the offer made by Christ was one of radical regime change, "an imminent revolution that would put an end to politics as usual."[4] He continues in this mode of thought, demonstrating how this new regime, one headed by God, was striking down the former self-serving status quo to build up an order distinguished by righteousness and justice.[5]

There are those words again: righteousness and justice. When the *basileia* of God is perceived, know that justice is present. So is the Righteous One.

Perrin convincingly claims that those who are poor—the very people to whom Jesus is preaching—would be most "jazzed by this kind of good news."[6] He further argues the society that first casts righteousness and justice into prison next throws into prison those in poverty. Further, Perrin believes that the more corrupt a society is, the less it will pay attention to wealth imbalances. So, who benefits the most if a just ruler, the Just Ruler, sits in the seat of power? People who don't have much going for them the way things are structured right now.[7]

To contextualize Perrin, we must first move beyond his setting of a singular society. On the borderlands, there is not one society, but two. Here, where societal and international power structures are readily apparent, it is also about how societies converge, the sociocultural dynamics of those who come to where these two societies meet, and who is allowed to cross from one to another. At the Border Church, the good news is proclaimed to and by people who are most in need. Before getting into the details of a theology of the *basileia* as displayed by the Border Church, let's first consider the rise of this exceptional expression of the *basileia* of God and the activist pastor who fought to make it a reality.

Even while watching the *basileia* and its activity at the borderlands, one cannot help but be aware of a different kingdom—an ungodly imperial force—slamming down its iron fist at the border. The United States, the nation I call home, has policies that show little welcome to migrants who cross the southern border in search of a better life. For a history of the legislative and judicial policies that the US has implemented toward migrants, I implore you to read Robert W. Heimberger's *God and the Illegal Alien: United States Immigration Law and a Theology of Politics.*[8]

This book is not a theoretical treatment of border and migration policy. Rather, this book contextualizes hopeful stories within an experience that is fairly characterized as unjust beyond belief. That said, I must draw your attention to two facts, dear reader. First, US immigration and border enforcement laws and practices are antithetical to the good-news teachings of Jesus as the leader of a new kind of *basileia*. Second, it did not have to end up this way and does not have to stay this way. Hold on to these facts as you move forward, but please do not forget entirely the backdrop of these hopeful stories.

A History of the Border Church

Dear reader, notice that I say "a history." My account is not a definitive history, nor is it a complete history; it's barely linear. Even still, as I relay events of the Border Church's past to you, I'm writing a *bona fide* history so you can appreciate the process by which the beauty of a flower arises from what once was merely a dead seed.

In brief, the Border Church started in the early 2000s based in the occasional acts of communion at the border led by Christian ministers in the Wesleyan tradition as a means to highlight the difference between God's call to unite and the US government's actions to divide and separate. Upon that foundation of communion, a community of Christians formed as the practice moved to a weekly model in 2011. From there sprang an active community of faith: those in Tijuana who minister with and to local displaced persons, a handful of faithful hikers that make it to the US side of Friendship Park every week (when there aren't other human or nonhuman factors keeping it shut) and a growing online English-speaking community in the US and beyond. Up to a hundred meals are served every Sunday in Mexico to a congregation whose core group is small but has impacted thousands of separated families, migrants, deportees, down-and-out *Tijuanenses*, and travelers from North America who come to see this beautiful community of faith and action for themselves. In sum, here at the edge of the border—and now online[9]—we work for the kind of *basileia* justice that Christ encouraged and foretold.

From the humble roots of Eucharist at the wall has arisen a church. To me at least, it is an authentic church. It's a church because Jesus is in the midst just as he promised. It's a church because it's a group of local believers who choose to congregate around the good news of Jesus. It's a church for me because at the end of the day, I'm a Baptist, and for us, in short, a church is a gathering of Christians who call themselves a church! For the past decade, a group of Christians has gathered and done just that, offering glimpses of God's *basileia* along the way.

The founder of the Border Church, one of the previously mentioned ministers in the Wesleyan tradition, is John Fanestil. This pastor and nonprofit CEO is an ordained elder in the United Methodist Church with a PhD in history from the University of Southern California. Recently, I asked John about the history of the Border Church. The following historical record is based mainly on what John recounted to me. His is a story of a man attempting to seek and understand the *basileia* of God on this slice of the border. It is a story of seeing God's sovereign and divine presence at work by breaking bread along and across an arbitrary national line.

John was a founding member of the Friends of Friendship Park (FOFP) when it began shortly into the year 2006. The impetus for the coalition was a new, more intrusive fence. The fence might have been new, but the ramping up of border enforcement was nothing new. It was years earlier that the militarization and weaponization of the southern border started. Year after year, funding for border enforcement has increased and continues to increase (nearly quadrupling between 2000 and 2015 from 1.06 billion dollars to 3.8 billion).[10] Meanwhile, tactical (read: militaristic) infrastructure spiked as well, starting in 1996 with Operation Gatekeeper under the Clinton Administration and reaching a pre-Trump spending high of 1.5 billion dollars in 2007 with nearly 700 miles of fencing.[11] According to one retired Immigration and Naturalization Services (INS) official, the Border Patrol that once was part of Immigration and Naturalization *Services* had become a counterpart to Immigration and Customs *Enforcement* (ICE) under the Department of Homeland *Security* (DHS) (italics mine) and, with veterans coming home from the warzones of Afghanistan and Iraq needing jobs, the nation's front lines with migrants were no longer being staffed by former Peace Corps members but hardened soldiers.

Here, in one slice of an increasingly hostile sliver of land stretching hundreds of miles from the Gulf to the Pacific, the DHS under the George W. Bush Administration was erecting a new barrier that made cross-border community nearly impossible. The goal of the United States was to split Friendship Park in half. This goal discounted the area's unique history, having once been declared Friendship Park as a binational meeting space in 1971 by then-First Lady Pat Nixon. Due to an intentional congressional giveaway of power, the executive branch had, for the first time under George W. Bush, been given nearly free reign (a different kind of *basileia*) on the border. No administration since has granted this rulership back to the legislators.

With a certain view of US national interests in mind, federal bodies like the DHS need not show regard for the history of a place such as Friendship Park or the families that so often had met there. The first couple of years of striving for Friendship Park and fighting the cutoff of its cross-border friendship and familial opportunities found little success. The government kept flexing its muscles, and its new fence kept coming. The militarization and weaponization of a line in the sand have become their gospel, despite the fact that its evangelists are agents of bad news more than good.

Two years into their work to save Friendship Park, in June of 2008, John, alongside others, concerned about access to family and friends at the border, attempted to have a communion celebration right there at the western edge of the border. According to John, many dozens of people came out on both sides of the wall to protest peacefully on that day. Another early FOFP member, Professor Jamie Gates of Point Loma Nazarene University, brought many of his fellow Nazarenes to an FOFP-led event. All went to invoke the message of unity in a place of division.

On that gloomy June day, the Border Patrol wouldn't let anyone approach the borderline or allow friends from the US side to join with friends in Mexico. Though parcipants were disappointed that the action couldn't happen, this physical blockade allowed for a different kind of statement to be made. John and Jamie are ministers from separate denominations, but both are fervently Wesleyan. Out of that shared tradition, they found the inspiration to change their Christian act of unity from communion to what is known as a "love feast." By doing so, all of those present could still partake in the bread and cup as an act of love, even if the elements weren't consecrated. So, in silence, they ate a meal of unity in response to imminent separation.[12]

The forty-plus people on the US side shared in this act in silence,[13] resonating with a recent *marcha de silencio*, which Pedro Rios of the American Friends Service Committee had organized—a style of activism that highlights the many unheard voices of separated families and that is still sometimes practiced at Friendship Park. Beyond silence, those who had been trying to keep Friendship Park open to the public were in shock; this was one of the first times that the Border Patrol refused to let anyone into the area at all. Up until that point, it was a place of few restrictions for those not attempting to immigrate without authorization. Johnn has exclaimed: "This had just been a place you went to and walked in." The change was stark.

After comparing notes with others in FOFP, John decided that he would simply go into the space on a routine basis and start serving communion. Eventually, the US government would have to kick him out. It would make a quiet yet formidable statement in line with protesters for rights hailing back generations. However, little public awareness was raised, given that the Border Patrol wasn't letting anyone into the park. It was not being brought to light by the press and remained relatively unknown to the populace, save for the most engaged. So, a statement desperately needed to be made for the families that would be separated in even larger numbers. They needed the public to take notice; they needed to get into what civil rights leader turned US Congressman John Lewis called "good trouble, necessary trouble."[14]

Early in August of that year, John Fanestil started celebrating communion in the binational space. The construction was underway, and the typical orange mesh fence began to find its temporary home between visitors and the growing permanent fence. Sometimes, John and friends would celebrate communion at the beach. Eventually, John made it a point to ascend to the top of Monument Mesa to celebrate (where we still celebrate), regardless of where the construction mesh was that Sunday. At that point, the Border Patrol took notice but did little to interfere, likely because to deal with the situation was more trouble than simply to let it go on unhindered.

John kept up this faith-based civil disobedience all the way until February 21, 2009, when a rather large binational choir was set to sing Gabriel Fauré's *Requiem in D minor*, where the border meets the sea. In a short video of that day, which is still available on YouTube, you can clearly see the demonstrators and the federal agents at odds with each other. In the video, an agent tells John that he is the leader and is responsible for the people there with him, to which John responds: "There is a calling higher than the law."[15]

With consecrated elements in hand, John moves forward to serve communion to those on the Tijuana side of the fence. That act of upside-down justice was too much for the so-called enforcers of justice. In the video, the Border Patrol agents can be heard demanding: "Move back!" Eventually, they handcuff John and one other man before hauling them, one by one, off the beach up the Monument Mesa. The physical barrier and agents make it impossible for any more people to even cross onto the recently seized federal land—in a way that stymies the efforts of the activists to make a display of the injustice at play in that place.[16]

This detainment was also a kind of farce.[17] John and others that day had been prepared to cross over and be arrested. The agents even threatened to arrest him. Still, John moved toward the fence and his friends on the other side. When they cuffed him and led him up the hill, he thought he was being arrested. Who wouldn't? But that wasn't the case. John got played. Technically, John had "voluntarily evacuated the space." He never got booked, and therefore, he was free to go, but by then, the protesters were slowly walking back up the beach to the north. So much for dramatizing injustice.

Nevertheless, John continued to go and serve communion. However, at this point, the feds would not allow him up to the fence, passively or otherwise. People kept trying to make a statement in one way or another. Daniel from FOFP was arrested once, but by and large, the concerned citizens' pressure campaign didn't have the momentum it needed to keep the Border Patrol engaged enough to change their strategy. Fence construction never stopped, and the face of the border changed forever (or at least until now).

Gardening in different soil did bear some fruit, though. Jamie and John entered into formal consultations between FOFP and Rodney Scott, who had been the head of the Imperial Beach Sector of the Border Patrol at that point and served as the chief of the United States Border Patrol in 2020 and early 2021. Chief Scott, in Jamie's same Church of the Nazarene, was open to having some measure of public access to Friendship Park. It was under Scott's authority that the metal mesh through which we pass the pinky sign of peace was approved and installed in 2011. Around this time, the US Customs and Border Protection started allowing for weekly Saturday and Sunday four-hour openings with a ten-person limit. Though the United States thwarted the initial goal of keeping Friendship Park as open as it had been, this new situation at least allowed John to continue his communion practice at the wall alongside families who depend on this park for face-to-face time with those on the other side.

From a weekly communion practice in defiance of the occupancy strictures placed unilaterally on a space intended for numerous binational uses, John had the chance to move into a new mode of practice, and so he did. Specifically, the 10:00–2:00 opening hours, he had heard were something that the Border Patrol had agreed to but did not follow when their whims changed.[18] This caused fears within FOFP that the Border Patrol would argue there was no need for the open space. So, John wrapped up the weekend opening hours of the park with the act of communion, thereby ensuring a presence in the park that would stand up to restless agents wanting to shut it down and a continued practice of the sacrament at the border.

This weekly presence started in November 2011. Only a few weeks later, John connected with another pastor, Saul Montiel, who had been tasked by the California Pacific Annual Conference of the United Methodist Church to work on immigration issues and have a cross-border ministerial presence. That ministry portfolio more or less meant that Saul's parish was the entire San Diego-Tijuana to Mexicali-Calexico span of the border as well as every immigrant household and neighborhood across southern California and beyond. As a Methodist, he might have felt like John Wesley, one of Methodism's founders, that the world was his parish. Here, he had "parishioners" from all around the globe.

In those early days, Saul would meet John near the border crossing in San Ysidro, where they would consecrate one loaf of bread and one cup of grape juice. Then, they would split the elements, only to bring them back together as close as they could at Friendship Park. More often than not, Saul would cross the border, and John would trek to Imperial Beach. Even this act served a familial purpose. While in Tijuana, the Mexican-born Saul would spend time with his family, eat tacos, buy the superior Mexican

Coca-Cola, and simply enjoy the time in the country of his and his wife's youth.

Early on, the Border Church was barely a church. It was more of an intimate gathering. Perhaps it could be called pop-up church, one with hardly any infrastructure or congregants at all. There was no ongoing community other than the pastors. Regrettably, in less than a year, Saul's position was eliminated due to budgetary concerns. Thankfully, Guillermo Navarrete, a member of the Mexican Methodist Church had risen as a natural leader by that point.

With largely Methodists leading the weekly event at the time, its makeup and practice had a very Methodist flavor. Yet, in John's estimation, it was not quite in the denominational fold enough to be genuinely United Methodist. More than that, the way that church policies work in Mexico, a body of believers cannot be a church unless they have a building, and we have only one wall—the border wall. Despite some support from the Methodists on that side, without a structure, it remained incomplete. Instead of Methodist, it was, perhaps, Wesleyan Light.

Now that many churches have experienced meeting outside and online due to the COVID-19 pandemic, maybe we all can rethink the idea of church as only what happens at a building.

Regardless, those origins eventually led to something broader and, I'd argue, a greater glimpse of God's justice as a part of the divine *basileia*. John and Guillermo are indeed quite Methodist, but they are also very ecumenically minded. Guillermo grew up in a different denomination, and John has spent many years as a minister working outside the church in the nonprofit world. In my thinking, this made the Methodist field ripe for an interdenominational harvest.

Before my arrival, the wider body of Christ was certainly already bearing fruit here through the work of Fr.

Dermot Rogers. This independent Roman Catholic priest labored alongside John for nearly two years on the US side. Dermot would preside at communion with or instead of John and share openly in the feast with him. The powerful act of a priest and a pastor coming together to serve the Eucharist embodies an act of defiance to all that would keep God's church from being one and all those who would stop God's *basileia* and interconnecting presence from coming fully. Though Dermot has since moved on, that spirit abides with us to this day.

The open communion table opened up to the less Wesleyan of us more fully once I was part of the leadership team. I had tried to be a Korean Methodist and then a United Methodist, but congregationalist polity was just too strong inside me. I'm glad to have met John Fanestil while on that part of my journey, and I am glad to be fairly Wesleyan in my approach to Holy Communion and other theological topics. Yet, after becoming American Baptist, I saw the intra- and inter-church nature of the Border Church in an unambiguous way. It's its own species of church. More than that, having seen up close the shifting sands of the local United Methodist Annual Conference's politics and budgets compelled me to argue for a wider reality, which had already been on John's mind and heart. We needed to be truly nonsectarian—coincidentally copying (or perhaps providentially parroting) the polymorphic nature of borders themselves.[19] The beauty is that, following the conscious move toward becoming an interchurch yet denominationally unaffiliated work, we have been able to invite more pastors and parishioners to take part in something that, at one time, might have felt "too Methodist" for them. It was too much of the "other." I am grateful that we have since then opened the table up even more. This fits the spirit of what is said nearly every Sunday, namely: "It doesn't matter if you're a part of this church or any church."

I can see in my mind's eye the fear that some of you may have on your faces. I cannot be with you to hear from you, but I want to assuage your distress as much as I can before proceeding. One apparent fear regards physical safety on-site. I have never felt unsafe there due to the so-called security issues. Many people gather at the place from all around. Beachgoers, tourists, and locals routinely walk by church happenings on the Mexico side, while beachgoers, bicyclists, and horseback riders can be found just north in the state park on the US side. The only fear I feel while there is for others—mostly those who are undocumented or fit some sort of perceived profile of a person who might be. Some agents have agreed not to check documentation papers in the space, but others still do occasionally. Even scarier, I have seen multiple times people jumping over or cutting and then running through the fence. I fear what kind of ice box awaits the vast majority who get caught.

Another fear is, one corresponding to all my talk of the Border Church being an actual church, is that of institutional validity. At the Border Church, everyone has the backing of their respective denominational bodies. Nobody is "going rogue" in terms of the work that each pastor is doing. Rather, the structures and budgets of the Border Church are not tied to the ebbs and flows of denominational life. More than that, the nonsectarian nature of the Border Church provides a safe space for people of a variety of traditions to be ministered to and to do God's work. It really is a beautiful thing!

Backing up a few years, it was upon Guillermo's ascension to the Mexican leadership that the infrastructure could start looking and sounding more like a church. Through Guillermo's work, as well as his penchant for using technology and certain kinds of structural patterns, the weekly communion, for the first time, had a different kind of growth potential. Specifically, his potential came in the form of a sound system as well as chairs, tables, and popup canopies. Before then, the intimate gathering of people at the wall had to be just that—intimate. In order to hear amid the sea breeze and beachgoers, gatherers stood huddled together just to hear. John looks back at that time and sees the beauty in that small gathering, similar to the upper room where Jesus met with the disciples. Even still, the science of sound and the mechanics of metal limited the potential to reach people in a very real way.

As the years have gone by, the sound equipment has grown and developed in both size and quality. From a single microphone held up against the micro-holes of the fence to wireless mics and powerful amps, the progress has made it possible to hear one another, even on those days when the park itself is closed on the US side.

In 2018 and 2019, when the US was needlessly fearful of migrant caravans and their fabricated "assault" on the southern border, we combined the tech of cell phones and microphones to share in the communion practice from farther away than ever before. During the flooding of 2020 and the pandemic of that year and beyond, we met via cell phone, Zoom, and a shifting array of speakers depending on the ever-changing conditions at the time. We couldn't even pass the peace with pinky kisses in person but only through computer or phone cameras. Regardless, Guillermo brought the tech and transformed the church. In doing so, he widened the rows for the seeds to grow. To this day, there's a small but active Border Church presence online each week. We call these participants our "cloud of witnesses." Over the course of the pandemic, folks have come from several US states and as far away as Costa Rica, the UK, and the Netherlands to stand in witness of what's occurring at the San Diego-Tijuana border—a true sign of the significance of what's happening in this small corner of the world.

Even as some pandemic fears subsided, sadly, Friendship Park remained closed week by week all the way up to the fifieth-anniversary celebration weekend in August 2021 and shows no signs of reopening in the near future at the time of writing and editing this book. The Border Patrol's excuse was that they did not have adequate staffing, which was odd, especially since we saw an agent sitting inside the Friendship Park gate vehicle virtually every Sunday in nearly the exact same way as he or she would have if that gate were open. By the time you're reading this book, I really hope the space is open again because a pinky kiss is bad enough when given through a wall. It's worse when it's through two walls and dozens of meters away.

As a simple communion practice was turning into what looked more and more like a church on the Mexico side, John invited a couple of families that had been a part of house churches in the past to set up a community of κοινωνία (*koinonia,* the New Testament word for fellowship and joint participation) on the US side, as well. They started in the summer, but by the winter, one of the families was in the middle of a divorce, and the other realized it was too much work to drag their small children through the sewage-contaminated muds of the river valley to get up to the park. Sadly, it didn't work out. It wasn't until COVID-19 forced everyone online that we finally started getting a sense of the *koinonia* from English speakers in the US and beyond.

One of my favorite memories of Friendship Park is from *La Posada sin Fronteras* 2017. Verna and I had our son Maximus only two months prior to this annual Latin-American celebration of the Christ child at the inn. After a relatively easy pregnancy, Max almost died in the delivery room and had to spend the first nearly two weeks of his life in the neonatal intensive care unit at the children's hospital. There, he was separated from his mama, who herself didn't fare much better and had to spend a week in the hospital, separated from her firstborn child. At that celebration, for Max to be in one of the most meaningful spaces for us as a family was a thrill. I set him up on a brick wall, where he could—with a little help—hold his head up and look over the waters of the Pacific.

Since then, Maximus and his sister Anastasia have come to Friendship Park and the Border Church with us when convenient—for us. For children, everything is hard, and everything is easy concurrently. All of life is new. The wonder of the world comes into less jaded hearts and minds. When I see my children or others in that space at the wall, I am reminded how the heavenly *basileia* is theirs. Jesus said we had to become just like children to experience it (Matthew 18:3). The children of Friendship Park go with the help of their family and seem to easily accept the beautiful realities of the place. In essence, their eyes are more open than ours to see the *basileia* even there. They don't need the readings, rituals, and rhythms adults crave to see God at work. Their hearts are open to the new because so much is new. As I ponder Max's eyes gazing in wonder upon the sea from above for the very first time, I was reminded that children are open to love through walls that keep us apart far too easily. In doing so, they show us the way to places and experiences that look like heaven. It's not always that the place has to be erected anew but that we need new lenses through which to view it.

The Border Church embodies the ongoing New Testament practices of teaching and preaching, community fellowship, breaking of the bread, and prayer (Acts 2:42). From my free church congregationalist point of view, this makes the Border Church a true church. Furthermore, by "sharing food with gladness and simplicity," we aspire to emulate the church of the apostolic age (Acts 2:46 CEB). While we have yet to see the kind of apostolic-style signs and wonders recorded in the book of Acts, we maintain hope in God for a sign of divine justice—ideally, the removal of this wall that divides and perhaps defines our church.

John has met many people at the fence throughout the history of the Border Chuch. These were borderlands people, binational in their very existence. Some were undocumented migrants crossing the border and showing up in Tijuana after being deported once again. Others were faithful fathers who came not only to participate in the church service but also to meet their US-based family members at the park whenever possible. John leads a community of faith made up of these borderlands people, including those who move comfortably and those who tread with caution on either side of the fence. We are a truly unique community of believers. If this isn't a reminder of our Christian nature not only in this world but also in one another, I could not tell you what is.

The *Basileia* of God Theologically in John's Voice and Mine

For John, the *basileia* of God is sometimes "fleeting" rather than a sustained sensation. John elaborates: "When these families show up and are reconnecting with their loved ones after talking on the phone or FaceTime for all these years, and now they're touching fingertips, that's incredible stuff. Right? And then, a half-hour later, they're back in their cars, driving back to Atlanta or wherever. The *basileia* of God manifests itself and appears but then disappears under enforcement." The polymorphic complexion of both the Border Church and the border itself is displayed for all to see.

John admits, "[The] power of the federal government is so obvious and so palpable that the reign [*basileia*] of God is sometimes hard to see . . . it's easily obscured by all the enforcement infrastructure and enforcement mechanisms.

So, you have to kind of go looking for it, you know, or have eyes to see it, so to speak. The reign [*basileia*] of God doesn't always quickly and readily supplant the reign [*basileia*] of the world."

John, sees occasional glimpses, perhaps in the form of unified singing on either side of the fence. The *basileia* is not fully present, nor is it sustained. It is still in the form of the mustard seed; the plant has not yet begun to grow. And yet, John's words could argue that the seedling has been growing there for years, even as John's understanding of it has also developed into something more significant and rich:

> There was real drama and power in the liturgy and in the breaking of the bread and the sharing of the cup. All the more so since we were commonly celebrating the sacrament alongside families who were visiting through the wall with loved ones at the park. Only occasionally did those families participating in the sacrament, but even when they didn't, they could tell that this was a way the entire community was rallying around them in support. So, the kingdom [basileia] of God started to look like something that included much more than just those who participated formally in the sacrament. A gathering of people—sometimes twenty, often fifty, and sometimes one hundred or more—would spontaneously collaborate to paint a picture of a community that transcended the world's divisions, as made so powerfully manifest in the border wall. So, I think it's fair to say that my conception of the reign [basileia] of God has expanded dramatically since I started working at Friendship Park, and I am guessing that it may continue to expand in the years to come.

For John, Friendship Park is a place with aspirations "of mutual encounter, of peace and harmony, of friendship and of communion," all aspirations that describe the *basileia* of God. A day at Friendship Park could be one of the ordinary things like "friends and families eating, walking, and swimming," if only the wall were to come down. John loves the Border Church and its prophetic presence that proclaims God's uncomfortable truth to human systems complacent with their privilege and power. Still, John's dreams would opt for a model of the *basileia* as it is in heaven over the continued practice of the Border Church at the San Diego-Tijuana border. "Thy *basileia* come" is more important than "Keep the church alive," according to John. In many ways, John's dream of a truly binational space within which people are free to do the ordinary and beautiful things, unoppressed by present barriers, could resolve the dissonance of *basileia* jazz that dominates our lives right now.

Weaving together my experiences and John's understanding of God's *basileia* at the border with this jazz metaphor calls three theological positions to mind: First, dissonance makes jazz better. Second, resolving the chord doesn't necessarily end the song. Third, the best jazz artists only *appear* not to know the rules.

New York Times music critic Anthony Tommasini reminds us that by incorporating the sevenths and even sixths of a chord, jazz fundamentally changed music. Instead of requiring them to go away, these dissonant notes give the chords and, therefore, the whole genre a unique beauty in its extra color and richness. No longer is the chord screaming to be resolved. It is different, it is complex, and it is good. Even as the chord resolves, the dissonant note or notes remain, and the resolution, though not total, still provides an acute sense of relief.[20]

Along the way, the dissonance can create a feeling of aversion, especially when we do not know its place in the divine melody that moves us continually toward a more significant whole. But, without these dissonant notes, jazz would not be jazz. I like jazz. Even in writing this book, there has been plenty of mellow instrumental jazz playing in the background. The *basileia* is like jazz. We know *basileia* and jazz when we are in its presence, even if our attempts to interpret or define God's *basileia* are inadequate. The ordinary, beautiful nature of community points to the extraordinary beauty of the true union which history is marching toward in Christ—when he will one day be "all in all" (1 Corinthians 15:28).

These dissonant notes can prove hard to interpret. Sometimes, the dissonance creates a feeling of aversion, especially when we do not know whether it's part of the divine melody—one that continues to move us toward something more significant and more whole. Again, it's like jazz. I used to like jazz a lot less. It wasn't that the music was terrible, but my tastes had not developed around it yet. If you don't like jazz, that's not a knock on you. It's just that the *basileia*, like jazz, is an acquired taste. And the more we listen to the music or feel God's *basileia* and presence, the more we can understand what it is, even if we can't describe it with speech.[21]

With jazz, the song may end when the chord is resolved, but it may not; the chord may not even resolve at the end. A chord resolved in a musical piece could just be a momentary reprieve before the next movement—one that could easily have more dissonance than the last one if it's a jazz number. "Four" by the Miles Davis Quintet, a fun, up-tempo jazz piece, is a good example. The Vince Guaraldi Trio's rendition of "Greensleeves," well-known for its use in the ubiquitous *A Charlie Brown Christmas*, also plays with dissonance and resolution.

The *basileia* of God is similar, as well. Since in more orthodox theological streams, we don't expect the fullness of God's *basileia* until the return of Christ, we don't experience the fullness or the end of the jazz piece just yet. Instead, John's glimpses of the *basileia* remind us of those fleeting resolutions. They are part of the piece that gives a brief sense of relief, but the music keeps moving forward in the right direction. It would be impossible to ascertain the beauty of the *basileia* without them.

Much like the jazz chord, with its sixths or sevenths or other dissonant tones, the *basileia* of God may never resolve in a way that makes perfect sense to us. When the dissonant chords of life resolve through God's grace, there may still be dissonance, even at the very end. A life well lived does not mean a life that is tidy. Too often, we flee from the dissonant discomforts of community life or other liminal spaces. The glimpses of God's kin-dom at Friendship Park serve as a reminder that there is beauty in the dissonance. God's *basileia* is at work through the ordinary, yet beautiful, rivaled against extraordinary, but worldly, powers.

The best jazz musicians are always breaking the rules. Talent in jazz music requires a gifted understanding, combining technical skills through repetition, knowledge of musical theory, practice, experimentation, and a mastery of the body as musicians connect with instruments. The better a jazz musician knows the rules and fundamentals, the more they can bend them to their instrumental will for the sake of a symphonic aesthetic.

I hope we can together conceive of Jesus as a jazz pianist for a minute. The notes that he played during his lifetime broke the many apparent rules of religious and civic life at the time. Yet, he knew the rules better than the scribes, lawyers, religious leaders, and the Romans, who had him killed. He had a lifetime of practice following the Holy Spirit.

He bent the rules for the sake of the good news: the *basileia* of God. It was coming. It was present. It is coming. It is present. If the good news is a piece of music written by Jazzy Jesus, it is one that still thrills, still sends chills, and still sets people at a standstill. Even the cadence of jazz reminds us that there is a movement about this whole thing.

So, too, is there a continual movement toward God's good end as we catch glimpses along the way.

That is the *basileia* of God in jazz.

NOTES

1. The most used translations of *basileia*, "kingdom" and "reign," are fraught in some sectors because of the inherent patriarchy and imperialism, respectively. I believe the terms still have valid usages in Christian theology, because the good news of Jesus the King entails a *basileia* defined by a justice-oriented systemic power reversal. However, to avoid needless offense and instead invite the reader into a broader conception of this fundamental Christian reality, I leave *basileia* mostly untranslated in the book.
2. Michael Bird, *Evangelical Theology* (Grand Rapids, MI: Zondervan Academic, 2013), 52.
3. Nicholas Perrin, *The Kingdom of God* (Grand Rapids, MI: Zondervan Academic, 2019), 36.
4. Ibid., 162.
5. Ibid.
6. Ibid.
7. Ibid.
8. Robert W. Heimberger, *God and the Illegal Alien: United States Immigration Law and a Theology of Politics* (Cambridge, UK: Cambridge University Press, 2018).
   In brief, Heimberger argues that the US bases its immigration laws on a stream of migrant law that started in medieval continental Europe and the British Isles. This legal tradition considers the immigrant, especially the one from far away, as an "alien." From there, the legal tradition developed into one wherein the "alien" became unlawfully present by default. The most recent update on this stream of US law has been to consider the neighbor an alien (and therefore principally breaking the law when on this sovereign territory). With this legal history in the background, it is no surprise that we are so apt to "other" the very people Jesus told us are our neighbors.
9. Find the Border Church online at https://www.borderchurch.org/.
10. ACLU, In National Network for Immigrant and Refugee Rights, "Border Militarization Policy and Corporate Outsourcing," https://nnirr.org/drupal/border-militarization.
11. Zach Turner, "Border Militarization and Corporate Outsourcing," *NNIRR*, June 23, 2015, https://nnirr.org/drupal/border-militarization.

12. Kennan Ferguson, "Silence: A Politics," *Contemporary Political Theory* 2, no. 1 (2003): 49–65, DOI:10.1057/palgrave.cpt.9300054. Vincent Jungkunz, "The Promise of Democratic Silences," *New Political Science* 34, no. 2 (2012): 127–150.

13. Other silent protests are worth noting here, including The Negro Silent Parade of 1917, civil rights sit-ins for the sake of access to lunch counters, and Colin Kaepernick among other athletes who take a knee during the national anthem on behalf of those harmed at the hands of the police.

14. John Lewis, Twitter Post, June 27, 2018, 8:15 AM, https://twitter.com/repjohnlewis/status/1011991303599607808

15. FriendshipParksdtj, "Feb 21–Attempt at Bi-National Communion San Diego/Tijuana Border Friendship Park," YouTube, March 14, 2009, https://www.youtube.com/watch?v=DyCeSRDLeuk&feature=emb_logo&ab_channel=FriendshipParksdt.

16. Ibid.

17. Such games provide that agents of enforcement, not just protesters, engage in performance and spectacle.

18. Much more could be said here about the intersection of immigrant racialization and people of different migratory and racial identities coming together as ordinary people in extraordinary circumstances. For the purpose of this work, however, it only need be stressed that our work seeks to unite people across a spectrum of identities in contradistinction with the prevailing cultural and nationalist forces that both intentionally and unwittingly divide based on those identities.

19. Andrew Burridge, Nick Gill, Austin Kocher & Lauren Martin, "Polymorphic Borders," in *Territory, Politics, Governance* 5, no. 3 (2017): 239–251.

20. Gabe Johnson, "Dissonance: Jazz," *The New York Times*, May 30, 2014, https://www.nytimes.com/video/arts/music/100000002837167/dissonance-jazz.html.

21. Many Christians believe in silence as a means into prayer and union with God. God is here in these speechless moments beckoning the believer to unity with the Divine. Even for those less mystically inclined, the practice of Christianity can rightly be described as transrational, and the move of the Transcendent goes beyond any tongue-tied testimony.

CHAPTER 2

PHOTOGRAPHIC FAITH

To look into the eyes of family members meeting at the border fence is to see into their souls. The faces of these families reveal the tenderness and vulnerabilities of their hearts and minds. To document the highs and lows of these embodied souls—from playful laughter at a sister's expense to heart-wrenching last goodbyes in this mortal life—is to document, in ways more raw and powerful than this author can muster with the Roman alphabet. So exceedingly powerful and intimate are these souls, rendered naked in these moments, that photographic faithfulness sometimes means putting the camera down to best do justice to the people experiencing the moment. Even more so, the unfettered emotions, tied to the harsh realities, must not be exploited. These souls—and the bodies in which they reside—are exploited enough. So, a camerawoman of faith uses wisdom to know when and where to shoot or what not to show at all.

With a sweet, aging smile and a keen sense of what she wants, Maria Teresa Fernandez, often referred to as MT, is, first and foremost, a photodocumentarian. While MT's artistic ability and the composition quality of her work are obvious even to the most novice viewer, what makes MT's work so important is its longevity and consistency.

Maria Teresa was at Friendship Park back when communion could be passed through the old border fence, and she was there to document it. She has continued through the new barriers and policies of the administrations of Bush, Obama, Trump, and Biden. Excluding Friendship Park's shutdown on the US side due to the COVID-19 pandemic and subsequent refusal by the Border Patrol to reopen it, MT documented has come out nearly every weekend to speak faithfully through images. As a Latina immigrant herself, whatever becomes of migrants at this section of the wall, MT has continued to document whatever she can.

This chapter consists of a story of MT's faithfulness as well as theologizing on her photographs. In the subsequent paragraphs, you can expect to see and read about families separated by inhumane immigration laws, the physical infrastructure (aka the wall) that assists the US government in keeping families apart, and the Christian practice of communion which invites all into the knowledge that we can be one family through the work of God here on earth.

Maria Teresa's Borderlands Take

Maria Teresa makes no secret of her immigration status. During the near lock-down days of the COVID-19 pandemic, we sat together for a virtual meeting. She reminded me that she could have easily been a part of those families whose images fill memory cards, clouds, and hard drives. Luckily, MT had the right "fit" to cross legally and live freely in the United States with friends and family. Instead of being stuck, like so many families in so many images, she was free to traverse back into Mexico whenever she felt like it to see her family south of the fence.

Maria Teresa does more than just see herself in the families that she documents; her work pays down a debt she believes she owes to them. She does not see herself as any better than these families, yet she has the kind of life they can only hope for—one defined more by the border region than merely the border fence.

Maria Teresa prefers to call the metal monstrosity that's filled her frame for years a "fence" as opposed to a "wall," in part as a reference to her first borderland photo project, entitled "*Cerca de la Cerca*" ("Near the Fence"). By calling it a fence, MT is also using the language of the Border Patrol. "Fence," "wall," "*cerca*," and "*muro*" are somewhat interchangeable. That said, Trump's famous call to "Build the wall!" has a visceral force that "Build the fence!" simply lacks.

Maria Teresa was led to Friendship Park first by the terrorist attacks of 9/11. She recounts it this way: "One of my instructors took me there because this class was supposed to take pictures in Tijuana to study the city through images." However, after the border shut down in response to the attacks, the professor "decided to take us to the area of Friendship Park. It was my first encounter with the place."

She didn't find any attraction to the US side of Friendship Park at first because there was less to photograph and also less access to the fence itself. Instead, MT documented the many objects and activists on the Mexican side. "I started documenting everything that I saw on the fence," she says. In 2007, says MT, "I started to visit Friendship Park, and that's when I found Dan [Watman] with his projects: salsa classes, poetry readings, and yoga classes. It could [and, in fact, did] hook me. That place really attracted me, and I started visiting and documenting what was happening in that place, too." Eventually, Friendship Park became her greatest muse. There, she also found an ability to connect with what was happening on the northern side of the fence.

For over a decade, MT has made it her practice to visit Friendship Park at least once a week. When the road is open to cars, she tries to go twice a week, usually on Saturday morning and Sunday afternoon, during binational communion. Maria Teresa is an unwaveringly yet soft-spoken evangelist who faithfully partakes in the communion feast for the Eucharistic event taking place there. Some Catholics who come to the fence to visit family fear receiving communion without confession. As a Catholic, MT invites them to a table of full inclusion covered by public confession. She lets them know that the offering of the bread and the cup is for everyone—and that "everyone means everyone."

Maria Teresa explains this reality with a story:

> There was one moment when there was a family there, a couple. I asked the lady: "Do you want to receive communion? You can come. It is open. It's an open ceremony." The lady quickly responded: "No, I can't. I'm living in sin. I'm living with that man; he's not my husband." So, I said: "Don't worry about it. We want to receive all of you. You are well-received. It doesn't matter who you're living with or not."

Whether she knows it or not, MT is echoing John and Charles Wesley, whose spiritual DNA is pervasive at the Border Church. As have many within his Christian lineage, Wesley and other early Methodists like him taught that the communion sacrament draws us, no matter where we are, to Christ. Transforming his own communion experience into poetry, Charles Wesley wrote:

> "Oh what a Soul-transporting Feast
> Doth this Communion yield!
> Remembering here thy Passion past
> We with thy Love are filled."[1]

John Wesley also speaks in prose on the work of communion in its partakers' lives: "I showed at large . . . that the Lord's Supper was ordained by God to be a means of conveying to [the recipients] either preventing, or justifying, or sanctifying grace, according to their several necessities."[2] In short, communion is a gracious and divine medicine for all that ails the human soul.

While MT knows of Wesleyan teachings only through overheard snippets and does not confess to be a theologian, she readily sees the heart of what she participates in at the wall: unity. She refers to communion's welcoming act as "a beautiful part of the service that unites all of us. You [the minister] always say before it starts that everybody is invited to be a part of communion—without pushing. It's beautiful."

The nuances of centuries-old debates between Abrahamic monotheisms or more recent but still abiding conflicts within Christianity itself do not matter to MT. This photographer's lesson on unity continues:

> I'm a Catholic. I don't practice, but it's become a service to do whatever I do at Friendship Park to be with the families, guide them a little bit if they don't know what to do, and to listen to you [the minister]. And I don't care if that's Methodist or evangelical or Muslim or Baptist because the community that you and John have made in the US over there with different priests or ministers or whatever you're called—I accept all of you. The families don't care about the divisions. So, anything that is a part of the moment in the communion is just beautiful. And that's it. It's become part of my Sunday service.

To her, in this place of unjust division, the beautiful thing is the unity found there. It is Holy Communion that displays that reality best for her. It does for me, as well.

Binational Beach Days of Yore

Pictured is a man with his two daughters. Let your eyes rest on it for a few moments. How do you feel when viewing it? When it was taken on July 21, 2007, the man was stuck on the US side of the fence, likely due to his immigration status. The odds are that he either had a work visa that didn't allow him the "luxury" of going back to Mexico to see his family or that he was in the US without acceptable documentation. He represents a statistic of

Father and Two Daughters on Beach at San Diego-Tijuana Border Fence.

economic realities in low- and middle-income nations and a rigid US immigration policy unwilling to look at the real people and families impacted by these realities. Whatever his status, he is more than a statistic. He is a father who has left his home to provide for the people he loves most.

The man at the fence holds his younger daughter in his arms; she is the picture of innocence. However, from the photo's US vantage point, she remains faceless. There are those who would argue that this father doesn't deserve to be *here*; it would be more challenging to argue that she doesn't deserve to be with *him*. He is her dad, after all, and the same political pundits, Christian or otherwise, that so often spout off about how "illegals" and "aliens" ought to stay away, also wax eloquent about "family values" and the "importance of fatherhood." The truth of this family defeats the punch of that argument. If a father is working to provide for his children, a nation away, and still makes an effort to visit them when he can, it would, indeed, be difficult to argue that he is not a worthy father. Yet, it has been decided that he is not worthy of seeing his child beyond these few square meters of beach, now cordoned off from the public by DHS officials and through a fence.

I don't feel less secure when I see this image; I can bet neither do you. Not only do I perceive a man with arms around his small child, but I also see the tender touch of a father and a daughter who is inching toward adolescence. In a world of predatory men, she stands along a border where myriads of young girls find themselves illegally trafficked. I see a comfort on her face; her eager expression reminds me that it does not always need to be this way. This image portrays a hopeful relationship of light.

The beauty makes it all the more heart-wrenching to know that this kind of cross-border contact is no longer available to fathers and their daughters. Due to increased federal enforcement infrastructure and action, the once frequent beach picnics no longer happen.

Maria Teresa captured many moments like this. Her camera captured the various poses and postures of family and others who would gather there, circling round in bright beach chairs or under striped umbrellas nearly blown over by the sea breeze. All the while, they shared food and fellowship across a fence that had openings just large enough for petite persons to pass through for hugs and play. The Border Patrol watched but rarely intervened.

Decades prior, much of the border was like this. In fact, it was even more porous. Thousands of Mexican fathers would cross for a harvest; they nearly always went home. Even though their income came mainly from the US, their lives were in Mexico. Vijay Prashad, in *The Karma of Brown*

Folk, says: "The United States wants these [immigrant] workers for their labor, but certainly not for the lives they must import as well."[3] The US policies have been designed to allow migrant labor to happen in and on US soil but not to allow laborers to fully become a part of US society.

As a father who has traveled for work myself, I can empathize with these parents in the smallest of ways. The sadness of a father leaving his family for several weeks or months at a time is immense, but the time would eventually end, allowing for *papá* to return home. He didn't have to stay once he crossed the border because his status didn't allow him to return; he didn't have to illicitly haul his entire family across the border with him out of fear of detention or deportation.

Migrant mobility no longer seems to be tolerated on any sort of just scale. Instead, we, as a so-called Christian nation, are actively destroying the families while preaching that they represent divine realities.

Build That Wall! And Then a Few More

People gather on the US side of the border wall at Friendship Park on other side of Tijuana lighthouse.

Maria Teresa took this photo on September 24, 2017. What you can see in this image is a church at the wall. What you can't see in the image is the second wall. It sits right behind MT, and it holds our view in this area of unbridled governmental control. As of just before the pandemic, only ten people were allowed to gather in this space, which once easily fit hundreds. Only ten individuals—less than in the above photo—and even that number has fluctuated over the years, always according to the whims of an unelected, multimillion-dollar federal agency. Ten people. I find that hard to believe. Then, flooding and the pandemic shut it down completely. As the road dried and COVID-19 restrictions were easing, the number remained at zero. I find this unconscionable.

Before the United States controlled it so tightly, Mexicans were able to travel freely here. Prior to the Mexicans were the Spaniards. Preceding those colonizers were the Kumeyaay—a tribe of indigenous people who lived in this area for thousands of years before European conquest. There were likely others before the Kumeyaay, as well—all of whom traveled along this coastline whenever necessary. The first Western ranches built here barred indigenous people from access to the mouth of the river.[4] Volumes more could be said about the injustice of our Western imperialist expansion against indigenous and mestizo peoples here. In short, we, as Americans, took this land as a spoil of war; little by little, we have made it into a war zone once again.

The border monument once made this little stretch of the border a place for tourists to visit the edge of the two nations. There were US settlements and hoped-for towns, which either got washed away by the rains or eroded by the passage of time. Eventually, there was barbed wire. A ramping up of border enforcement came next. Between the increased border enforcement efforts of the Clinton years and those of the second Bush administration after 9/11, there was more fencing along the San Diego-Tijuana border than had been erected during Operation Gatekeeper in 1994. During that anti-immigrant operation, the government initiative to curb illegal immigration in the San Diego region turned large sheets of metal, once used for temporary military landing strips in Vietnam and during the Gulf War, into a miles-long fence stretching almost out to the Pacific.

Returning to MT's photo, I ask you to look at the pictured congregants and family members. Squint like we must do when we count those on the other side. Strain your ears as if to attempt to listen to them. The senses were not made for this kind of setup. God did not intend for big chunks of metal to come between us. And yet, we gather here as a separated people of God. We come to a steel wall to turn it into the table of the Lord. Instead of allowing a false justice to dictate our practice, we recognize the *basileia* of God and Christ himself as the center of our work. In doing so, it is the rule of divine justice and faithful love that wins the day. Therefore, we spiritually and symbolically change a symbol of evil—the rusty steel barrier—into a table of welcome. We hold hope that the symbolic change, one day, becomes a tangible one. With our confidence in God, we also know that the eschatological hope we have for the *basileia* on the border (and in the world) will not disappoint.

Theologically, you may already understand that a church is more than a building and that the church is more than an earthly institution, but have you been a part of a congregation up against one wall? I imagine not too many have. Instead, as people of faith, we typically worship within four walls. We worship with the privilege of modern heating and air conditioning and the less modern luxury of a roof over our heads. Even with the near-paradise weather along the California-Baja California border, the modest infrastructure of a building makes corporate worship much simpler.

We don't have that luxury at the Border Church. In essence, we have only one wall—the wall between us.

A building keeps us comfortable enough to pay attention. It keeps us and our things relatively safe from pests and thieves. The sanctuary, or the equivalent space for other congregations, is a place of special significance for the congregation. For this reason, the space is intended only for church-specific activities.

In the Sanctuary Movement of the 1980s[5] and the New Sanctuary Movement[6] happening today, church activities include taking in foreigners as friends of the church. Each night, some migrants call the sanctuary itself home. Alas, at the border, we only have one wall to lean up against, and I doubt our federal "landlords" would stand for it anyhow.

At the Border Church, what we do seems to, in fact, run counter to the design of the space itself. With armed law enforcement on the northern side of the fence and advanced technology peering down at every moment, it is clear that we are barely welcome. If it weren't for the Friends of Friendship Park, the public would likely have lost access to this slice of human connection along an otherwise alienating border. Yet, the design of Friendship Park on the US side, as you can see in the image, is not welcoming, nor is it beautiful, save for the beauty brought to the space by the people who visit.

In a place designed to keep people disconnected, we use spiritual realities to overcome physical barriers. My mind's eye sees images of others taking up this universal and timeless motive, seeking to bridge divides across time: Black and white freedom riders and peaceful protesters in civil rights actions of the 1960s, the Black Lives Matter marches of the current era, ecumenical dialogues seeking repentance and reconciliation from institutional churches that have not always spoken the truth with love, and biblical images of people from all tribes, tongues, and nations worshiping the Lamb. Even more, I see simple acts of love: greetings exchanged, meals shared, and lives devoted to easing pain and sharing the light of spirituality with any and all who cross paths.

It's been some time since anyone from the Border Church had to cross an obviously demarcated line to celebrate communion at the border. The day to be brave may come again, but until then, we will continue to meet at our little slice of an ever-looming, ever-changing wall. It is not the structure, but the Spirit, that makes it holy.

A First *Hola*

Proud new father introduces newborn to grandparents through the border fence at Friendship Park.

One of the moments with the most unfettered joy in a person's life may be that of welcoming a grandchild into the world. Parenthood is a wonder, but it is enigmatic—and hard. On the other hand, grandparenting is a walk in the park, particularly in cultures that prioritize nuclear families over extended family units. This is a child you can be proud of but who doesn't come with a great deal of day-to-day, night-after-night obligations. The child is a source of happiness, without the obligations of daily—and nightly—care. At least, that's how grandparenting looks from my point of view, as a parent of two toddlers.

In this photo, taken in August of 2018, the camera shoots from just behind and to the right of a proud father and his new baby; we can see the side profile of his smiling face and the chubby cheek of the child. Instead of a pinky kiss, the father offers the child's toes for an embrace through the fence. As small as this child is, he's still too large to fit through the tight mesh, also richly displayed in this photo. In the background, I recognize hands wiping away an emotional display of tears—the result of a context I find far too familiar.

What can we not see from this vantage point? The other. In this image specifically, the absent others are the child's grandparents—the *abuelos* meeting their *nieto* for the very first time. We cannot know, based on the image alone, their reactions—whether they are smiling or crying. We cannot be certain even of their presence in the captured moment. Only the human expression, and, for me, prior knowledge of the scene, gives any clues to our mind's eye of what is present on the other side of the fence. In this image, the father's expression intimates the presence of someone else—someone of great importance in his and his child's life.

The grandparents' absence in this image indicates something more extraordinary: a commentary on the current media ecosystem, fed by clicks and views to keep its revenue stream coming. As a result, journalists see incentives in posting stories that capture lazy readers, grabbing our attention, and ultimately urging us toward ad clicks for things we do not need. In turn, this incentivization structure and the human nature of the consumer upon which it was founded is far more likely to churn out stories that evoke a strong reaction—whether positive or negative. Beyond taking an honest look for ourselves, if we were to take a true look at the statistics, we would see that negative reactions to content are stronger, more emotional, more likely to win out over the level-headed response, and, therefore, more likely to yield more engagement. Whatever turns up the temperature is more likely to compel us to click, and sensationalist headlines are more likely to stick in our heads. I am not exempt from this, and neither are you.

Let me reiterate this point: what sells are the headlines and hot takes which cause our senses and feelings to go "bang." Apply this logic to what we are doing right now, and you can see why this book is intentionally emotionally startling. It is not unlikely that some level of an emotional "bang" prompted you to buy this book and kept you reading to this point.

Yet, the sensationalist stories that sell rarely paint a complete picture. There is so much more to the image of the border than the "trauma porn" that blinds us to the hope and goodness that can be found there. This book, whose foundation is rooted in God's *basileia* and the justice of that reality, paints a picture of hope.

At the border wall, two generations came together to welcome a third. This little story of a little person with little toes is a story of faith—faith in what is to come. Life goes on, and family life will continue. The future is brighter than it was before this new life was a reality for these unseen grandparents. It is a story of faithfulness. It is a story of love. Whatever the story, it is a small story, but it is an authentic one. You will never ever read this story in a newspaper or see this story told on cable television. It is ordinary yet beautiful.

Maria Teresa's photos reveal, to me, the wonder amid the mundane: moments of joy and sorrow that expose the wonders of human existence that, if not for this fence and all it represents, would be reserved for a family photo album or a person's other small, personal, and private spaces.

Exposure to this intimacy is a beauty to behold, yet it is unnatural. I am grateful for the opportunity to bear witness and experience the goodness of humanity instilled by the Creator. Still, I would rather these moments be shared with me across more culturally traditional walls instead of at this one, constructed with steel and unwelcome.

A Last *Adios*

Distraught woman seen through mesh of US-Mexico border fence at Friendship Park.

Gaze into these eyes. I see sadness. What do you see? How do you feel? Maybe you want to look away in shame. Perhaps you want to comfort this lady or change the circumstances that have caused this overwhelming grief. Some of you may find yourselves even fighting the compassion you feel with narratives of assumed disgrace. Our reactions say more about us than anyone else.

Some of the most challenging stories at Friendship Park are the goodbyes. Here, the goodbyes are ever-present. As I mentioned earlier, I occasionally give my final benediction and *adiós*, while walking backward out of this federally operated space. It is not difficult to recognize a family saying their goodbyes; it is an easy read because of how drastically their affect changes. A general pattern of a family reunification day at the park includes great expectations on the way. There is a pattern to family reunification day at the park. On their way into the park, families bursting with exuberance reunite, then they settle into a conversation, and finally, their goodbyes—goodbyes that always carry a sense of loss.

Loved ones meeting at the border will likely not see each other again for several months. The goodbyes are especially heart-wrenching when families live far apart. Families traveling from either country's outermost regions or farther are not uncommon during these reunions. Members on both sides make special plans—sometimes having saved up for years—to turn this desire of a fenced-off family reunion into a nearly tangible reality.

The time and distance raise the stakes of every reunion. The longer the wait has been, the more likely it is that the next reunion will be the final goodbye. Underlying health conditions necessitating a final goodbye could be as simple as an aging body that may not be roadworthy for much longer or as complex as a diagnosis of terminal cancer. The former is pretty stark. The specter of the latter haunts each reunion with the threat of a possible prognosis of a few months; it does not bode well for another reunion after this one. Whatever the reason, it is in these moments that a devout member of the Border Church documents these goodbyes with her camera.

So, what should we learn from these families, barred from hugs and handshakes, saying goodbye in such a nonideal situation? I want to highlight three things: 1) the Christian value of family, 2) the use of resources for something good in the world, and 3) the impermanence of this life.

An ancient Hebrew worship song attributed to the one and only King Solomon declares: "No doubt about it: children are a gift from the Lord; the fruit of the womb is a divine reward" (Psalm 127:3 CEB). Though I admit that the thought of the teenage years may give me some pause, I firmly believe this statement to be true.

I know too many families whose wombs are not biologically fertile; I don't intend to leave them out. The blessing of families goes well beyond the nuclear family of 1950s white culture or even the Greek-influenced households of the New Testament era. On the borderlands, this is an obvious truth. Though not the majority, families of all stripes—whether God-given or chosen—show up for each other.

Regardless of the make or model of a family, there is a spark of the Divine there. After all, the primary relationship within the Trinity, as found in the New Testament, is between a Father and Son. We could go on and on about the theologically understood differences between the economic Trinity and the immanent Trinity; instead, consider the words from One to the Other at Christ's baptism: "You are my Son, whom I dearly love; in you I find happiness" (Mark 1:11 CEB). The greatest gift to the Heavenly Parent was the Human Child of God. A loving God found happiness in that relationship. We can only strive to create the same level of intimacy, love, and joy in our familial relationships; however, the same Spirit of God that brought that message to Jesus in the form of a dove was the One that hovered over the waters at the dawn of creation and has led the faithful up until this very day.

When a family shows up for a dying loved one, they offer the best gift they can to that person—themselves. In the faces of loved ones, the sick can receive happiness because of their shared love. The dying can receive care from the people in this world who mean the most to them. They know they may not have such tokens of care after these moments. Gratitude abounds even as loss looms. May we be so grateful.

I imagine most readers would not hesitate to go looking for a checkbook or credit card to make a similar trip, if necessary. I am less convinced that the reader would do the same to alleviate other sufferings of this world, which I would argue are just as crucial to the Heavenly Parent looking down at all God's children.

I am skeptical about this in the reader because I know about this lack in the author. The vast amount of suffering in this world is too often a din I would just as soon drown out with entertainment or work than have to suffer—even if slightly—to alleviate. Yet, in this place, I am confronted with suffering face-to-face in a place where my cell phone signal barely works and there is, undoubtedly, no cable or internet. At this sacred site, separated but whole families at the border give up on the succor of temporary pleasures to see each other and care for the dying as they go.

As we turn our gaze from the border to our own lives, I start to wonder about backyard ethics: What are you doing for the sick and dying who are not your friends and family? What are you doing for these fellow residents of the *basileia*? In your circles, who are those made other, and how do you respond to people experiencing suffering, whether apparent or not? It's obvious my nation has made non-citizens of different races so other that they can't come here, but what about that different kind of person who gets under my skin enough that I push them away without regard to their struggles? I admit it is far too easy to take up attractive or low-maintenance causes and dismiss others, but the invitation of the *basileia* is for all, regardless of our predisposition to them.

Throughout my lifetime, poverty has been headed in the right direction—down—and yet people still have been dying from preventable diseases at alarming rates—rates that sadly saw an about-face because of COVID-19. So, the scenes of struggle so readily found in the borderlands are not confined to this space. Each of us has neighbors struggling, and we must love these neighbors in deed, not just word. The Leader of this *basileia* did, in fact, make such a command (Mark 12:31).

The Mexican families meeting here for the last time are doing so in a way that means they won't have some of life's little luxuries for a while—all because of the love they have for the family member who is dying. Though our love is not as perfect as the Father and the Son's for each other or for others in the divinely made human family, are not all equal before God? Does that not mean that the life we can save is worth giving up a luxury or two? I have been trying to cut out self-indulgences from my habits for years in order to be more faithful. It is challenging to stick with, but when I see the accumulating amount both of what I've saved financially and what I know about the bodies and souls I've helped save in places where my luxuries would feel like folly, I am anything but disappointed.

In the past, followers of the Abrahamic faiths acted out justice by routinely giving to those living and dying in poverty—whether or not they were a part of the synagogue, church, or mosque. In a turn of events that would shock our early faithful forebearers, this practice of almsgiving has largely fallen away within Christianity in exchange for unnecessary consumer habits and material goods. Perhaps, though, this kind of materialistic band-aid covers the deeper divisions we have with one another—divisions rooted in things like racism, xenophobia, and nationalism. These harmful isms are enacted through othering, oppression, and even genocide. Regardless of which injustice lies at the root of our unjust, self-seeking behaviors, God's *basileia* necessitates that we flip typical models upside down for the sake of the poor, beaten down, and forsaken.

When a family at the border says goodbye for the very last time, its members acknowledge the impermanence of this life; they begin to accept the truth of the impending loss. Life is temporary, and what it offers is not lasting. An earlier age of Christians often made use of the Latin phrase *Memento mori:* "Be mindful that you will die."

Die we shall, but we can live along the way. It's not just about the next life. If there is a hope amid the impermanence of this life, it takes a spirit of gratitude to find: in each and every moment, we can be grateful. Nothing will last forever—no relationship, no job, no struggle, no state of bliss, nothing. The world itself will come to an end, but along the way, we can find ourselves more and more skilled in living the life set before us one step at a time.

Church Elements at the Wall

Makeshift communion altar for Christian worship set up on US side of the wall at Friendship Park.

This photo, taken in April of 2017, shows the elements of the Border Church—or at least those that symbolize our Christian practice on the US side. There is a loaf of bread made from grain, a cup with juice from the vine, and, leaning against the same fence that now denies access, visual reminders of a more accessible age. All of this sits upon the makeshift communion table, made from a tattered mat lying atop dirty outdoor pavers. Beside these elements are the boots of a pastor whose pilgrimage to this site seeks a faithfulness to God and to fellow humans along and across the border. The humbleness of the scene may itself evoke memories of the humble nature of Christ's birth and earthly existence.

The photos among these elements show off better border times, a time when the fence had much bigger holes, a time that is no more. These photos represent something that is now untouchable; the photos themselves cannot be touched because they were stolen from Pastor John Fanestil's car. In stark contrast with the picture on the left, people can no longer freely and significantly engage in exercise—or anything really—in a binational way. Following the government seizure and transformation of the space into a US operation zone, only eight hours each week and the occasional gardening hours are available for any binational relationships to be pursued.

The center image is of Pastor John offering communion to a man in Mexico. This photo stands between the communion elements of that day and the new fence, which now makes such a cross-border act of solidarity in Christ impossible in the San Diego-Tijuana region. With the increased enforcement of federal customs laws, John's offer is not only impossible but, likely, illegal, carrying with it a possible arrest for smuggling. This photo, a memory of truly binational communion with one bread and one cup, sparks within the onlooker a hope that one day, physical proximity as a sign of unity will be possible again. We hope for a day when the fence is not just diminished but dissolved altogether. I do long for that day—one in which we can share in one feast together within two free nations.

The photo on the right is one of many people meeting, something that is no longer possible. During the initial months of the COVID-19 pandemic, the Border Patrol did not once open up Friendship Park to the public. Years before then, the ten-person rule on the US side of the fence disallowed many people from visiting there. Even the umbrellas and seats of the still image are a reminder of what has been lost. Now, no items of comfort can be brought in. This prohibition remains in effect for everyone, even for the elderly. The only chairs allowed in are wheelchairs.

Even the mat on which these items sit is all that can come with us to keep holy elements off the dirt and dust of the ground. This thin piece of cloth calls to my mind the attempts of the US government to keep out the "dirt" with a fence. On our side is what is holy, but *baja* (underneath) us lies what is dirty and unclean. Not unimportantly, the most sacred items atop the mat come from below it. Grapes and wheat grow out of the same dirt we try to keep off of them once they are in an easily edible form. So too, our current state of geopolitical and multinational economic affairs is impossible without workers from Mexico and the rest of the so-called developing world to keep our appetites momentarily sated with the consumer goods they produce. Their brown hands have already touched our stuff, yet they're not allowed in our places. It is as ironic as it is sad. The state of affairs in God's *basileia* is such that all done within its boundaries is made inherently whole and clean. No one is an outsider by mere accident of birth. All *basileia* work is inherently humane; all is holy.

Just off to the right of this communion table of dirt is a boot; this is the boot of a pilgrim pastor—one who walks forty minutes or more each way just to set up this makeshift altar to the Lord and remember once again the Lord's ultimate altar for us. Besides cowboy and hipster churches, my only knowledge of boots in the church is firsthand as a child growing up in Minnesota. Even though we kids often left our snow boots on in the cold, bleak winter, the preacher never did. Up above us all were loafers, at least. Much of the border, here included, is no place for the well-heeled. It's an environment where we need boots as rugged as the landscape that we slog through to get to church and footwear thick enough to (hopefully) keep the bite of a rattlesnake from penetrating if the serpent should happen to strike.

The Border Patrol agents wear boots as well. It is a mandate from the government that they do. They know the perils of the borderlands and need to be dressed ready for them. The migrants often can't afford boots. Typically, I see them in beat-up sneakers. Yet, they cross terrain at least as rugged as what we and the border law enforcement cross. Even in this, the disparity is stark.

The wise Border Church pastor chooses boots. The federal agent follows the order to do the same. The migrant has little choice but to wear what is already on their feet. Pages and pages of political science, anthropology, sociology, economics, philosophy, and theology can and should be written about such disparities. I do not want to dismiss that reality. Yet, I also must start with the theological truth that all of us in these three groups are equal under God's justice. The communion table invites us equally to be more like Jesus in the way of love and against imperial deceptions. Two millennia of theological debates haven't solved the question of how to enact the early church's practice of holding all things in common—sharing literally everything—for today, and I don't plan to solve it here. However, I hope that the inequalities among the trillions of dollars spent on defense and homeland security, the above-average wealth of a US clergyperson, and the characteristic poverty of the migrant are not an image of the reign of Christ here and now. More than that, I find myself convicted—even troubled—by the call to live for a Heavenly Authority here on the edge of the most powerful nation the world has ever seen.[7]

Most days, I'm a Baptist. Technically, I'm a Baptist every day as a member of the American Baptist clergy, but I *feel* like a Baptist most days. What I mean by that is I am not someone who holds a strongly sacramental view of communion—a robust Eucharistic theology. To condense centuries of theology into two camps is dangerous, but here goes nothing. Some Christians, such as Catholics,

Orthodox, Anglicans, Lutherans, and Methodists, view communion as sacramental and thereby a unique means of grace from God. Other believers, such as Baptists, Presbyterians, Pentecostals, and most nondenominational folks, have a different theological take. They prefer to think of communion as an ordinance—generally, one of two commands (along with baptism) from Christ himself that all followers of Christ must obey because he has ordained it that way. I'm speaking for myself here, knowing quite well that the Lord's Supper commonly divides us. Yet, if taking part in the Lord's Supper is sacramental in that it's a means of receiving grace from God, then I can sign up for that theology if I can also see a walk in the woods as sacramental or a day in silent retreat as imparting special grace or even changing a diaper as something potentially holy and wholly filled with *charis*.[8]

I remember once hearing a Greek Orthodox theology professor of mine waxing eloquent about the only means to building solidarity among differing churches, what's referred to as ecumenism, as necessarily Eucharistic. I liked what he had to say, but I don't think the theological messiness of our border communion practice is at all what he had in mind. Nevertheless, it is in the elements of Christian practice that meaning beyond them is conveyed.

I don't know many people along the border who read the works of Augustine of Hippo, nor do they need to. But in his philosophical theologizing, this fourth- and fifth-century Doctor of the Church teaches us how elements—more specifically, what he calls signs (*signa*)—point to something beyond themselves. In his thinking, there are natural signs—think smoke when it indicates there is a fire or the face of someone angry or sad—and what he calls conventional signs.[9] Such conventional signs, Augustine describes as "those which living beings mutually exchange to show, as well as they can, the feelings of their minds, or their perceptions, or their thoughts."[10] So, this kind of sign is an act or object that conveys meaning. This meaning goes beyond the action or object of the sign itself. People use a sign to give meaning, and then the people on the receiving end of the sign receive it through their bodily senses, usually sight or hearing. For Augustine, much of this early Christian semiotics, or study of signs, had to do with verbal language (*verbum*) as primary and writing (*litterae*) as secondary signs.[11] Yet, I don't think it's going over the line to bring this theology to the visual elements of the Border Church—those things that MT captures week after week with her DSLR camera. I dare say that Augustine would have added the pictorial to his own list of communicative signs if he had lived in an ancient culture as awash in images as our own contemporary one.

The elements in the above photo have significance in and of themselves. They may even have some categorical meaning in theology; bread and cup certainly do. Because the Border Church's intentions are, generally speaking, aimed more at *fronterizos*—and perhaps those who gaze upon this *frontera*—than other kinds of people, I seek to keep my interpretations of the signs within this circle. I realize there are concentric circles that go well outside of this one at Friendship Park. From a borderlands perspective, I also realize how boundaries—whether regarding things such as meaning or nation-states—are more of a construction than an objective, autonomous reality in their own right. This isn't news per se, but that it gets consistently reinforced deepens its realization in me. Regardless, I seek to remain in my own circle here, even as I hope it touches yours and captures some timeless gospel light.

One crossroads at which I may depart from the basic framework for Augustine's theory of signs and symbols is that I don't think all of them are intentionally pointing to the thing (*res*) beyond them in the exact way that the receiver is drawn toward that same thing. Even with the bread and cup of the border seen above, not all who preside at the communion table within the Border Church intention my own posited meanings consistently. Yet, I hope that all of my interpretations still exist as valid interpretative acts ready to be made for them and the other elements I describe.

The depth of meaning goes well beyond the intentions of the symbol giver. For the Border Church, it goes beyond the words on these pages. My interpretative framework is just too different from that of the people highlighted in these chapters and the myriads of visitors who have experienced the Border Church. The boundaries of whose interpretations are valid is a worthwhile question, but not one that I'm interested in pursuing in this book that's already filled with too many walls.

One of the earliest extant Christian documents outside the New Testament is the *Didache*, also known as the *Teaching of the Twelve Apostles*. In 9:4, the *Didache* declares a desire for the worldwide church to come together as one, even as the substance of the broken bread is one. Though separated by a fence, the loaf of Christ at the Border Church also proclaims that message in its own corner of the world. Here, where two nations meet and those from many nations travel great distances to find a better life, the unity of the worldwide church is proclaimed. We are acting as though we are one and seeking to be one. We cannot be one in the fullest sense of the word. No, we are separated by an infernal barrier intended with that very aim. More than that, language and cultural barriers prevent the fullness of unity proclaimed in the second century—or earlier in the Hebrew and Christian scriptures themselves. On top of it all, the doctrines we hold as Baptists, Methodists, and whatever else too often keep us from having unity as fellow travelers on the path to union with Christ.

Lord, help us. With all of this division, there needs to be a sign of the *basileia* to unite around. The sign of the bread whose grain comes from across the Americas is like the sign of the people who come from those same places. All point to the one Source from which we come and to whom we go.

As we look upon the one loaf in the photo, we cannot help but notice a wooden chalice next to it. In it is the fruit of the vine—squished, bleeding fruit. Like the broken flesh of our Lord and the torn-up flesh of a migrant's feet, the grape must have torn skin to become juice or wine. Beyond laceration, the grapes must be trampled, like the human rights of those who rightfully seek asylum. When we set out or hold up this cup at the border, we act faithfully toward the God who commanded the practice. We are also proclaiming the human significance of blood that connects us to God.

I have friends and colleagues who love the act of communion. I know others who can barely stand it—too visceral and violent. They do not see justice in it—much less God's presence or *basileia*. Yet, here at the fence, squeamishness about humanity's bodily nature and the embodied suffering endured by many—including the Savior—are hardly objects of scorn in the same way. In the faces of the separated, the abandoned, and the forsaken, I can almost see the suffering visage of Christ. Those same faces often light up with hope as they receive the bread and cup of communion. Jesus is there in their midst.

Together, the loaf and cup are ubiquitous in Christian historical and contemporary practice. Without the body and blood, Jesus would not have been truly human. He could not have actually died in the ultimate act of love. Like in some early heresies, the God-Man would not have been a human at all but instead a phantasm or a cosmic spirit. At the border, everyone is all too aware of their own humanity and the contingent frailty of flesh and blood. Yet, in proclaiming the goodness and reality of the quintessential

Human, Jesus, faithfully announced the fundamental good-ness and validity of every person's human existence. God made a good creation. Sure, sin has marred it, but the im-age of Christ in humanity is not lost. The corresponding goodness still lies deep within our ensouled frames. Like MT, let us bear faithful witness to what God has and is do-ing in this world of ours.

NOTES

1. Ole E. Borgen, "No End Without the Means: John Wesley and the Sacraments," *The Asbury Theological Journal*, 46, no. 1 (1991): 68, https://place.asburyseminary.edu/cgi/viewcontent.cgi?article=1502&context=asburyjournal.

2. Ibid., note 55.

3. Vijay Prashad, *The Karma of Brown Folk* (Minneapolis: University of Minnesota Press, 2000), 87.

4. Barbara Zaragoza, *San Ysidro and the Tijuana River Valley* (Charlottesville, SC: Arcadia Publishing, 2014), 17.

5. Rhonda Shapiro-Rieser, "The Sanctuary Movement: A Brief History," Center for Religious and Spiritual Life at Smith College, March 1, 2017, https://sophia.smith.edu/religious-spiritual-life/2017/03/01/sanctuary-movement-history/.

6. Judy Bolton-Fasman, "Helping the Stranger: The New Sanctuary Movement," *Jewish Boston*, March 20, 2018, https://www.jewishboston.com/read/helping-the-stranger-the-new-sanctuary-movement/.

7. See Leisy J. Abrego. *Sacrificing Families: Navigating Laws, Labor, and Love Across Borders* (Stanford, CA: Stanford University Press, 2014) for a deep dive into pan-American transnational, separated families and the effects such a divided state has on the family members, including the children.

8. *Charis* is Greek for "grace." In the New Testament, as here, it's usually God's grace in view.

9. Stephan Meier-Oeser, "Medieval Semiotics," *The Stanford Ency-clopedia of Philosophy* (Summer 2011 Edition), ed. Edward N. Zalta, https://plato.stanford.edu/archives/sum2011/entries/semiotics-medieval/.

10. Augustine: *De doctr. chr.* II, 3 (1963: 34): "Data vero signa sunt quae sibi quaeque viventia invicem dant ad demonstrandos quantum possunt motus animi sui, vel sensa aut intellecta quaelibet." See Jackson 1969: 14f, Meier-Oeser 1997: 24–30.

11. Meier-Oeser, "Medieval Semiotics".

CHAPTER 3

THE CROSSING OF HURT AND HOPE

Week after week, the Border Church sees migrants and would-be asylees on its southern side. As migrant waves wax and wane and US budgets rise and fall, our weekly work with migrants awaiting entry into the US shifts in various ways and needs to be done with a spirit of openness to change. Regardless, every Sunday is an opportunity to commune with people on the move from all over the world.

The following story is of a woman from Central America. Her story is as unique as her beautiful smile, but it is also a doorway into a life of hardship. Here's your chance to peek inside injustice and still see hope. May the story bring you a deeper understanding and a greater impetus to act.

Karla is a Honduran migrant. She is the mother of three children, but that count only includes those still alive. She lives in a *colonia*[1] in Tijuana with her husband and two of her kids. The remaining child survivor was given up for adoption in Honduras to keep her safe. Karla's story of getting to where she is has become one of trauma, loss, recovery, and hope. Her whole demeanor is one of faithful resilience and hope in God. Of all the stories in this book, this is the one that brings me the most sorrow and carries with it the greatest foundation for joy. That is because Karla is the very kind of person the Border Church seeks to serve.

Karla fled Honduras for the United States in 2018. She was part of the most infamous of recent caravans, arriving during the Trump presidency. Her life in Honduras was not one of affluence. In fact, she could barely get work. Like many in Central America, Karla worked as a farmer whenever she could. With the harsh weather, grueling working conditions, and neocolonial exploitation, among other issues, doing farm work in a place like Honduras is not very similar to the storied notion of agriculture in the American heartland. Arguably, it's more of an American hades.

Honduras has high levels of poverty and inequality. More than 48 percent of its residents live in poverty, and rural areas have a 60 percent poverty rate. Only 11 percent of the population is middle class. There is also a lot of violence in Honduras, with more than thirty-eight homicides per 100,000 people. Compared with the rate of twenty-nine per 100,000 intentional homicides in Mexico[2] or five per 100,000 in the United States,[3] it becomes obvious why someone like Karla would so desperately want to leave.[4]

Karla is more than a statistic, though. So were her family members who walked into a violent death. Her father, mother, and brother were all killed. Karla didn't want to be next. She had already lived on the streets starting when she was eight years old. She had already tried to ease her troubled mind with hard drugs, becoming an addict at age fourteen. She wanted something better for herself.

Between her childhood and her journey north, a group of Christians from a local Honduran church gave her a home to stay in and showed her the way of Jesus. Their act saved her life. She fully believes that Jesus saved her soul, too. Sadly, the Christians who offered Karla a path to freedom from addiction through Christ didn't have the power to keep her safe from the men who murdered her family. So, she left.

She joined the 2018 caravan with music in her heart. As someone who loved Jesus now, she learned songs about him in the popular *alabanza cristiana* (Christian praise) genre. Many people may recall the political furor over this massive group of travelers, but the songs of praise in some parts of the caravan were not shown in the media. The media coverage stirred up white fears of brown bodies on the move, but it didn't represent this caravan as people of God on the move.

Karla didn't have to wander forty years in the wilderness as the Israelites did, but she did have to wait once she crossed over to her own promised land. It wasn't the Jordan River but a fence that a pregnant Karla had to pass through on December 3, 2018. Before too long, she was picked up by US federal agents in San Luis, Arizona, and she tried to claim asylum. As happens all too often, the agents didn't believe her claim. Instead, they threw her in *la hielera* (the icebox). More than that, they didn't believe her when she cried about "*un dolor que no se imagina*" ("a pain you couldn't imagine"). Deep within her body, something was physically wrong and causing her to scream out in anguish. The agents who were witnesses to her cries did nothing to help this pregnant woman as she pled with them about an incredible amount of pain that she could not stand. They countered her cries with statements that not only dismissed her pleas but also ignored her humanity: "*Eso no es nada*" ("That ain't nothing").

After Karla was transferred to the High Desert Detention Center in Adelanto, California, someone with the power to act finally listened. So, on the last day of the year, she was admitted to the hospital. Instead of ringing in the New Year with friends and family, Karla miscarried and lost her baby on a holiday that ought to be for celebrating new beginnings. To add insult to injury, this mother, who fled her country to make a safe home for her family, had her hands and feet shackled to the bed like a criminal, even as she suffered the unspeakable loss of her baby. At her most vulnerable, Karla's valley of the shadow of the death of her unborn child came with no human rod or staff of comfort, only criminalization and chains.

The injustice is unreal. But it is also all too real for many who flee to the US for help and instead are treated horribly. History shows the grim realities of our government's treatment of migrants. Whether it's the deportation of US citizens under President Dwight Eisenhower's Operation Wetback, the cold, cramped holding cells or "iceboxes" constructed during the Obama administration,[5] or the more than 5,500 children separated from their families under the Trump administration,[6] officially sanctioned maltreatment of migrants on US territory is nothing new.

Karla spent six months in the United States. Her modern-day dream of an exodus to a land flowing with milk and honey came true in the scantest of ways, for she was barred from partaking in its bounty. Unlike the Israelites, who called Canaan their homeland after years of struggle, Karla was kept out by a government with force more extraordinary than anything in Joshua's ancient conquest stories.

Karla eventually found herself in Tijuana, a city she had never known prior to her arrival. Such a disorienting journey is not uncommon for asylum seekers. Thousands of would-be asylees are sent back from the US across the border to Mexico, often to regions other than where they had crossed in the first place. During Trump's "Remain in Mexico" scheme, the asylum seekers were forced back across the border before even being granted a full hearing. Of those in this program, formally called the "Migrant

Protection Protocols," as few as 0.1 percent of those seeking asylum received it. That number is virtually nonexistent compared with the 20 percent asylum approval rate of those who remained in the US while they tried to fight for their legal rights.[7]

Many migrants and asylum seekers are fleeing the terrifyingly likely prospect of being murdered. Others seek to escape poverty and the brunt of global economic injustice, which has some roots in past US corporate and government interference in other sovereign territories. When I imagine what I would do in these situations, I would most likely flee. You probably would, too. I can only imagine what I would then do once the so-called "shining city on a hill" pushed me back down. What would I do for my family if the actions of the country I thought would be a safe haven left us caught between a fence and a hard place? I may well stay right where I ended up. Karla did precisely that. She got stuck in a new place and chose to remain. Here, she found the Border Church as a new expression of God's *basileia*.

As I mentioned above, Karla loves praise music. I am filled with awe when I think about her description of how the worship songs work in the people coming to worship at the border: "*Se siente una gran fe que traspasa el cielo.*" ("It feels like a great faith piercing the sky.") She continues: "*Se siente una gran fe, algo emocionante. Algo muy lindo, se siente hasta el otro lado [de la frontera]. Se siente aquella emoción. Es hermoso.*" ("It feels like a great faith—something exciting. Something very lovely, you can feel over to the other side of the border. You feel that emotion. It's beautiful.") It's beautiful, indeed.

Karla usually cannot attend the Border Church services because our meeting spot at the wall is too long of a walk from her *colonia*. The cost of taking a taxi there is completely unaffordable. Still, Karla fondly remembers meeting the people who introduced us, Pastor Guillermo Navarrete and Robert Vivar (whose stories appear later in the book), as well as others from our core Mexican group. She describes the Border Church service that she witnessed as *"muy buena"* ("very good") and *"excelente"* ("excellent"). Here, she found that we speak the truth and provide *"comida a las personas"* ("food for the people"). She connects the two by saying: *"Hay personas que también andan necesitadas, de la Palabra y del estómago."* ("There are individuals who also have need for the Word and for the stomach.")

In Karla's words, when we worship at the border, we overcome the national barrier:

> *En el Faro se siente que no hay fronteras, aunque esté ese muro ahí, se siente que no hay fronteras cuando uno está ahí. Se siente que los dos lados están unidos. A pesar del muro, se siente que no hay fronteras. Es una emoción muy bonita; ojalá que algún día quitaran ese muro.*
> (At El Faro, it feels like there are no borders, although this wall is there. It feels like both sides are united. Despite the wall, it feels like there are no borders. It's a very lovely emotion. I hope that one day they will remove that wall.)

Karla is a farm girl who loves creating things and who has a home complete with dogs, rabbits, and birds, which she has referred to as a "jungle." Karla describes God's creation with insight that I wish others would take to heart: *"Cuando Dios hizo los cielos y la tierra, no hizo fronteras. No dividió nada. Él hizo la tierra perfecta. Nosotros, los seres humanos, hemos destruido la tierra."* ("When God made the heavens and the earth, he did not make borders. He did not divide any of it. He made the earth perfect. We human beings have destroyed the earth.")

The divine wisdom of justice, faith, and hope in Karla's words rings true, but no one at the Border Church can claim responsibility for her profound thoughts. The work of God's *basileia* was underway while she was living in Central America and even on the perilous path north to our border. She found these virtues on her own, through other people of faith, and from the Faithful One before she ever worshiped at the fence that held her back from what she once thought was her land of milk and honey.

For Karla, to be a Christian is to demonstrate faith *"porque con la fe se mueven montañas"* ("because with faith, mountains are moved"). Karla has great faith in God. She believes in God because, in her words, *"Me ha sacado de muchas situaciones."* ("He has lifted me out of a lot of [bad] situations.") She says that faith is what brought her from Honduras to where she is today: *"La fe en Dios me traído hasta aquí; me da fuerzas."* ("Faith in God has brought me here; it gives me strength.")

It is through Karla's faith and hope in God that she was able to pray to have her children with her so that she could have the chance to be *"una madre ejemplar"* ("an exemplary mother"). It was through this faith and hope in God that she has been able to start going back to Honduras for her children *"uno por uno"* ("one by one").

Karla's hope and faith have led her to believe in God's promises. She says:

> *Dios me prometió, de que él me iba a dar a mis hijos nuevamente. Y uno por uno, mis hijos han venido para acá. Ahora tengo a [lo de siete años y] la de doce años aquí. Solo me falta una. La fe en Dios es muy grande. Le voy a decir algo, perfectos no somos. Perfectos no somos. Todos cometemos errores, perfecto solo Dios. Yo lo único que sé, es que, con todo y mis errores, Dios me ama y sigue amándonos. Y voy a tener a mis tres hijos, porque Él me lo prometió. Yo sé que voy a tener a mis tres hijos de nuevo conmigo. Aunque sea uno por uno, pero ahí voy.*
>
> (God promised me that he would give me my children again. And one by one, my children have come this way. Now I've got [the seven-year-old boy and] the twelve-year-old girl

here. I'm only one short. Faith in God is very great. I'm going to tell you something; we're not perfect. We all make mistakes; only God is perfect. All I know is that with everything and my misdeeds, God loves me and continues to love us. And I'm going to have my three children because He promised it to me. I know I'm going to have my three kids with me once again. Even if it's one by one, but here I come.)

Here is the love of a mother and the faith of a servant of God. It is the hope in God that I yearn for and wish were always conceivable in my own life. I have faith, but Karla has the type of faith that moves mountains. Her faith is not sight totally, but it is coming to be. It is the substance of things hoped for; it is the evidence of things not yet seen.

May the story of Karla enrich your life as it inspires courage and action. Give assistance to migrants fleeing an unjust system. Give until it's uncomfortable. Tell your church's governing board and local elected officials it's time for a change. Be willing to defy unjust authority if they don't relent in being part of the problem. If that sounds scary, at least do *something*. If a story like Karla's story doesn't compel you to act, I am unsure anything will.

Contextualizing this personal narrative within US immigration history shows that despite its self-described label as a "nation of immigrants," this country has never had an open-door policy. Its immigration policies have always been tied to an underlying eugenics mission and an unjust economic system.

Immigration continues to be a major factor in the US political discourse. It was shortly after the end of Trump's presidency, which was marked by the harshest rhetoric and action toward all kinds of immigrants, whether they were family members of people already in the US, economic migrants, asylum seekers, or climate change and political refugees that President Joe Biden set forth a piece of legislation on the first day of his administration that included major reforms of immigration law.[8] This proposal, plus early executive orders that reversed much of Trump's harshest immigration policies, offered some hope to migrants as well as to the millions of undocumented immigrants already living in the United States, yet US immigration policy still does not welcome enough people like Karla.

The Kumeyaay people called the lands on which I live and work their ancestral home for approximately ten millennia, yet they are not in charge of the policies that govern what is now a binational region. Rather, it is people who have come since then, largely the descendants of European immigrants, who hold the reins of power today.

Even as migrants from southern Mexico, other nations in Latin America, and beyond come to Tijuana, immigrants continue to arrive in the United States whether they have governmental permission or not. As shown in the table below, the total population of the United States at the end of fiscal year 2017 was 322 million.[9] Of those, roughly 87 percent, or nearly 280 million, were native-born citizens. The remaining 44 million persons, approximately 13 percent, live in the United States but were born elsewhere. Therefore, this nation now has the highest percentage of foreign-born residents since the 1910s,[10] though still lower than the majority of Organisation for Economic Co-operation and Development (OECD) countries.[11] About one-quarter of the people who make up this monumental number are undocumented immigrants.

Table 1: US Population Fiscal Year 2017[12]

Native Born US Citizens	278.8 million
Naturalized Citizens	20.7 million
Legal Noncitizens	13.1 million
Unauthorized Immigrants	11.3 million
Temporary Visas	1.7 million
Total US Population	322 million

Table 2: Main Source Countries/Region of Immigrants[13]

Fiscal Year	S. or E. Asia	Mexico	Europe & Canada	Caribbean
1960	338,328	575,902	8,208,811	193,922
1970	573,102	759,711	6,553,312	675,108
1980	2,258,351	2,199,221	5,992,431	1,258,363
1990	4,578,724	4,298,014	5,095,233	1,938,348
2000	7,528,999	9,177,487	5,736,328	2,953,066
2010	10,336,238	11,711,103	5,616,086	3,730,644
2015	12,112,272	11,643,298	5,620,290	4,165,453

	Central America	S. America	Middle East	Sub-Saharan Africa
1960	48,949	89,536	141,013	13,696
1970	113,913	255,238	194,719	47,747
1980	353,892	561,011	324,850	129,946
1990	1,133,978	1,037,497	466,626	264,775
2000	2,026,150	1,930,271	771,999	690,809
2010	3,052,509	2,729,831	1,041,970	1,326,634
2015	3,384,629	2,918,029	1,274,241	1,716,425

In 2015, Mexico was no longer the leading source of migrants living in the US. The largest percentage of immigrants came from South and East Asia. However, when we combine the number of immigrants from Mexico with the number of immigrants from Central America, Latin America still represents the highest percentage of immigrants.[14]

In the fiscal year 2017, nearly 1.13 million individuals became lawful permanent residents (LPR). In all, 46 percent were male, while 54 percent were female. Within this same LPR category, more than half a million immigrants received an adjustment from a less permanent legal status, while almost 600,000 were new immigrants. The general categories of immigrants that year were as follows: nearly 750,000 came through family and immediate relatives, employment brought 137,855 immigrants to the US, refugees and asylum seekers accounted for 146,003 people, and 94,563 people came for other reasons. The top country of origin for new lawful permanent residents was Mexico.[15]

It is hard to see the justice or *basileia* of God in these statistics, which is one reason why we turn to stories where they can be found—even within unjust economic and immigration systems. The story of Karla, I hope, demonstrates that there are real people behind these numbers. Real people like Karla need us to respond as citizens of the *basileia*. We need to respond as its Leader would. So, how would Jesus respond with hope to migrants, including refugees and asylum seekers?

THEOLOGY

In *Toward a Theology of Migration: Social Justice and Religious Experience*, Gemma Tulud Cruz, who holds a PhD in theology and is also a migrant from the Philippines to Australia, offers three especially valuable points: one bread, one body, and one people.

Christ gave one bread. We are one body. God has one *basileia* people.

ONE BREAD

Since contemporary global migration patterns display a desire by millions to relocate for a better existence, according to the author, the reality is that people move in search not of pleasures but of daily necessities. In Cruz's words, they search for bread. Only one world exists that we currently can call home, and this world has limited resources.[16]

Cruz writes: "The physical, material, or economic motivation for people on the move, in a world that is turning more and more into one global village, reinforces the Christian idea that we share, and ought to share, one bread."[17] Cruz argues that the common good makes clear the meaning of "one bread." Specifically, within Christianity, the legitimate rights of communities and individuals must be bound up in everyone's common welfare. More than that, all things are, at their core, God's. Every single thing that God gives us is under a social mortgage. Instead of being a payment or reward, it is a gift. Every divine gift stems from God's gracious hospitality to us as guests in the created cosmos.[18]

In light of the "one bread" notion, Cruz argues that migrants and refugees challenge us to share the earth and whatever resources we have on it. Sitting here in National City, California, right now, I can look out the windows and see what would be considered a poor neighborhood by US standards. Yet, these standards are well above the global mean. This shows that our consumption habits in this country are incredibly high by world standards and that, in general, our resources surpass those of other nations and cultures.[19] My neighborhood—and yours—has untapped wealth (material or otherwise) to share. By sharing our resources, we are sharing the one bread.

Bread is a global symbol of physical nourishment and survival, but Cruz asserts that bread is a religious symbol as well. She considers how bread is an integral part of the Christian faith and a symbol of spiritual nourishment and discipleship. The Hebrews received "bread from heaven" while in the wilderness, for example (Exodus 16:4-21). In this biblical narrative, Cruz sees a potent reminder that we all need nourishment and that we all need to share in God's bounty equally.[20]

Jesus presented himself as both the "bread of life" in John 6:35 and the giver of bread in Matthew 14:13-21. You may recall that one of the last acts of Jesus before Judas's betrayal was to break bread with the disciples. Cruz connects that act with the actions of Christians who commemorate Jesus Last Supper through Holy Communion. For Cruz, this is the zenith of Christian worship.[21]

The existence of Karla and others like her challenges us to share our bread—literally and metaphorically. It is not originally ours, after all; it is from God. Too often, we go about life unmoved by the reality that the same globalized systems from which we buy our provisions hurt the people producing what our appetites crave. Hopefully, this broken global system offers ways to share the bread in our bank accounts. Though we have leaps and bounds more in terms of resources, few American Christians even give the 10 percent tithe the ancient Hebrews did.

Now more than ever before, I can care for Jesus as I care for "the least of these" (Matthew 25:40-45) not only in my community but around the world. There's more wealth in this century than there has ever been before. If you're living in an English-speaking nation, you're likely in the top 10 or 20 percent of the wealthiest people alive within the most affluent epoch ever. That's one kind of true hope—as long as we share our bread with others.

A greater hope comes in the form of Jesus Christ. Hope is an unrealized expectation for the future, but the hope of the *basileia* isn't merely about the future. It can and must be realized in ways big and small right now. We can *do good* now. The global pandemic worsened the situations of many of the poorest in our world, but our dollars, time, and prayer can do wonders to alleviate worldwide suffering and to save real lives.

ONE BODY

A theology of migration also reminds Christians that we are one body. Cruz acknowledges that she is not the first to put forth such an idea. The first we know of was Paul, who wrote in 1 Corinthians 12:12-27 that those "who are many" are "one body." Paul grounds his idea of the oneness of the body in the "one bread." Thus, he inextricably links this one body and one bread for all Christians. Cruz goes further in relating that oneness to the contemporary innovations of technology in transportation and communication, which both tie the world together.[22]

Cruz asserts that migration, especially from the Global South to the North, underscores the one-body idea of Christian theology. If one part of the body moves, the whole body can feel it. The body image of 1 Corinthians 12 centers Cruz's affirmation that all members of this body are essential and that special consideration must be given to the weaker parts.

Within this framework, Cruz argues that the body of Christ is unwell because some segments are saying to others, "I don't need you!" She goes on to argue that the vulnerable parts of the body, including migrants, bring with them cultural and economic resources. Moreover, they can fully form their parishes and faith communities within the universal church or body. That can happen in one's new home as well as in one's land of origin.[23]

Every week at the Border Church, we hear the awe-inspiring words of Jesus in two languages: "*Esto es mi cuerpo*" means "This is my body." The "this" is the one body; it is the one bread. Though we come from many walks of life, we are united in the one body of Jesus. Whether the person partaking in that gift of Christ's one body is a Honduran, a Mexican, a Canadian, or anything else, God makes them all one. The Maker of the *basileia* knits together everyone who comes just as this same Creator knits together each body in the womb (see Colossians 2:2 and Psalm 139:13). All who come there in the body of Christ are indeed one. A person's status as a citizen, a resident, an asylum seeker, a refugee, or a deportee does not impact their status as a member of the one body. We are one.

ONE PEOPLE

The third takeaway from Cruz is of the Christian notion of one people within the milieu of people on the move. She sums up the oneness of humanity in light of migration as providing "a way of rediscovering and recovering a sense of universal humanity based on mutual dependence and common destiny as citizens of a single world."[24] She argues that, based on Pope Benedict XVI's *Caritas in Veritate*, the doctrine of the family extends to all humans; all are family members, and all compose one people.[25] Furthermore, the doctrine of the Trinity roots Christian thought in pure relationality and absolute unity.

Part and parcel of Trinitarian thinking, Cruz sets forth the idea that oneness does not mean losing any individual identity; it means radical interpenetration. As a result, Christ's prayer that "all may be one" in John 17:21 is made possible. Beyond that, the people's oneness marks the oneness of the church's catholicity (universality). For Cruz, this catholicity is not something that gets negated by lack of authorized documentation or that stops at the border. Instead, it spreads beyond fences and walls to reach foreigners and migrants and make them strangers no more. This is because all are part of one human family and, as Christians, one pilgrim people.[26]

Here we are on a journey, following the hope of Christ with the faith we have in Christ. Here we move forward together as one. Sometimes, it seems like we are moving like the Blob of mid-century horror movies or, at best, Batman's nemesis, Clay Face. Our boundaries are imprecise. Our directionality is awkward. Yet, we continue. We go on with hope and its biblical conception as confident expectation, not merely wishful thinking, knowing that our end goal is the *basileia* of Christ now and forever. In short, our hope now and in the future is Christ.

NOTES

1. A *colonia* can be defined, though not exclusively, as a neighborhood of a large Mexican city.
2. See https://data.worldbank.org/indicator/VC.IHR.PSRC.P5 ?locations=MX.
3. See https://data.worldbank.org/indicator/VC.IHR.PSRC.P5 ?locations=US.

4. "Intentional Homicides (per 100,000 People)–United States." Data. https://data.worldbank.org/indicator/VC.IHR.PSRC.P5?locations =US.

5. Cindy Carcamo, "Immigration Fact Check: 'Who Built the Cages?'" *Los Angeles Times*, October 27, 2020, https://www.latimes.com /california/story/2020-10-27/presidential-immigration-debate-fact -check-and-who-built-the-cages.

6. Kevin Sieff, "Separated at the Border, Reunited, Then Separated Again: For Migrant Families, Another Trauma," *The Washington Post*, January 31, 2021, https://tinyurl.com/287z7fnn.

7. Gustavo Solis, "Remain in Mexico Has a 0.1 Percent Asylum Grant Rate," *San Diego Union-Tribune*, December 15, 2019, *https:// tinyurl.com/2p8ptues.*

8. Rebecca Morin, Rick Jervis, and Rebecca Plevin, "Biden Immigration Proposal Looks to Roll Back Four Years of Trump's Hardline Policies," *USA Today*, January 20, 2021, https://tinyurl. com/3h8ut3vn.

9. Maria Pimienti and Chesterfield Polkey, eds., "Snapshot of Immigration 2019," National Conference of State Legislatures, March 29, 2019, https://www.ncsl.org/research/immigration/ snapshot-of-u-s-immigration-2017.aspx.

10. Jie Zong, Jeanne Batalova, and Micayla Burrows, "Frequently Requested Statistics on Immigrants and Immigration in the United States," Migration Policy Institute, last modified July 10, 2019, https://tinyurl.com/2hu7marf.

11. OECD, "Stock of Foreign-Born Population in OECD Countries," 2020, https://data.oecd.org/migration/stocks-of-foreign-born -population-in-oecd-countries.htm.

12. Pimienti and Polkey, "Snapshot of Immigration 2019."

13. Ibid.

14. Ibid.

15. Ibid.

16. Gemma Tulud Cruz, *Toward a Theology of Migration* (New York: Palgrave Macmillan, 2014), 153–154.

17. Cruz, 154.

18. Ibid.

19. See Center for Sustainable Systems, "US Environment Footprint Factsheet" 2020, University of Michigan, http://css.umich.edu/fact sheets/us-environmental-footprint-factsheet.

20. Cruz, 154.

21. Ibid., 154–155.

22. Ibid., 155.

23. Ibid., 155–156.

24. Ibid., 157.

25. Ibid., 158.

26. Ibid, 159.

CHAPTER 4

THE LOVE OF A MOTHER

Tania and I meet in the office of the Border Church. We chat in the back of a large, open room in which volunteers are giving legal aid to migrants trying to move north of the border. A line of lockers separates us from the rest of the area. In this echoey space, filled with the noises of hopeful and fearful families, Pastor Guillermo attempts to make us as comfortable as possible. Both Tania and Pastor Guillermo agree that I should use the comfy desk chair, while Guillermo offers Tania a hard chair at first—more of a portable shower bench than an actual chair. Eventually, they find a hard-backed chair like you would find in a Sunday school room.

Being offered the most comfortable chair and treated as an honored guest results in a deep sense of personal discomfort as my privilege is made so clear. However, in these cross-cultural encounters, I have learned not to allow my "woke" white guilt to refuse something given from the heart. So, when they insist, I comply. In that act, I hope I allow the ground of justice—God's *basileia*—to abound in our midst.

Tania was born in Jalisco, Mexico, in 1986. She immigrated legally to the United States as a very young child and grew up in Los Angeles, the only city she calls home. She has a teenage daughter in L.A., but because Tania is a deportee whose ten-year ban only recently expired, she cannot visit or live with her child. Tania's life is unique, but it is not unlike many deportees living on the borderlands and hoping to return to their families and to the US cities that their hearts call home.

In Spanish, the word for "history" and "story" is the same: *historia*. To tell a true story is to recount history. What you're reading right now is not a history book, but it contains history because it is about the lived realities that borderlands people are experiencing in this historical moment. To add context to these *historias*, I'll give a brief history of the borderlands.

In prehistory, the Kumeyaay people lived for roughly twelve thousand years in the land where Mexico and the United States of America meet. In 1542, these indigenous people had their first contact with foreigners from beyond their shores when the Spaniard Juan Cabrillo sailed into what is now known as San Diego Bay. Later, the Spanish colonized the Kumeyaay's land. The first local colony was built in what is now the Mission Valley neighborhood of San Diego, named after the Catholic mission that undergirded its inception. Its founder was a Spanish Franciscan priest named Junipero Serra.[1]

After a brief period under Mexican rule starting in 1821, California was split between Mexico and the United States by the Treaty of Guadalupe Hidalgo on February 2, 1848, at the end of the Mexican-American War.[2] The US also took other Mexican lands as the spoils of war. This division underscores the present-day line through the middle of what is now the San Diego-Tijuana border, the second-most populous binational metropolitan area in North America with 5.5 million inhabitants.[3]

The first customs houses in the area were built in 1873 on the US side and in 1874 on the Mexican side. Not even a decade later, the first overtly unjust and racist US immigration policy, the Chinese Exclusion Act of 1882, was signed into law, which planted the seed of border enforcement as a form of surveillance and control. During this time, the situation worsened when Chinese immigrants were smuggled into the US by way of Baja California.[4]

Since then, the situation has not gotten much better for immigrants' rights under either of the two main political parties in the US. The graph that follows illustrates the millions of migrants formally and informally sent away from the United States since the 1980s.[5] This visualization reminds me that the United States is not a welcoming country. The hostility toward migrants and immigrants is also apparent in the "Asiatic Barred Zone" of the 1917 Immigration Act, which essentially banned people from China, India, most of Southeast Asia, and nearly the entire Middle East from entering the United States. Our lack of concern for our neighbors has been apparent through various historical moments and policy decisions. For example, between 1942 and 1964, the Bracero program allowed millions of Mexican men to enter the US legally and work on temporary labor contracts. When this program ended, the US government staged a mass deportation of farmworkers—many of whom had lived and labored on US soil for years. Another example of hostility toward Mexican migrants was Operation Wetback during the 1950s, in which government officials deported upwards of 1.1 million Mexican nationals (and some US-born citizens). This was a racist reaction to the increase in Latin American farmworkers residing and working in the US. More recently, this blatant xenophobia is clear in the 1986 Immigration Reform and Control Act, which led to increased border patrol and punishments for employers who employed workers not legally authorized to

Foreigners Deported and Returned from the U.S.

Number of foreign nationals subject to formal deportation proceedings vs. informal returns*

- Foreigners deported - Foreigners returned

359,885

171,445

* A deportation is a compulsory removal following a court order, a return is the confirmed departure without such an order.
Source: Department of Homeland Security

statista

work in the US. This closed the door of gainful employment for many migrants seeking work. The 1990 Immigration Act disallowed judges from recommending against deportation, taking away case-by-case discretion and the possibility of mercy within certain kinds of criminal proceedings. In 1994, Operation Gatekeeper resulted in the walling off and militarization of the US-Mexico border in San Diego. Then, the Department of Homeland Security was established after the September 11 attacks, and the Border Patrol was subsumed into this newly created entity. The Secure Fence Act of 2006 resulted in the construction of an additional 700 miles of border fencing and further fortified the border against migrants, regardless of their motivations in coming. These are only a few examples of our long history of antagonistic and violent policies toward migrants. One more will suffice for this *historia*: President Donald Trump declared a state of national emergency in order to redirect funds from other military theaters to build his infamous border wall.[6]

As for Tania, more than just being counted among the millions and millions of deported people from the US, her history and identity are wrapped up in her being *una madre*—a mom. Her binational motherhood is why she's a part of this book. Tania is a representative of mothers (and families) separated by border and immigration policy. Tania is also a faithful part of the Border Church, so to know her is to become intimately acquainted with an important aspect of what this community is. Tania has been part of the DREAMer Moms who, before the pandemic, would converge weekly in Tijuana at Friendship Park for Border Church as well as for other activities that occurred on Sundays at the wall. Most of the DREAMer Moms are mothers of DREAMer kids who currently have federal Deferred Action for Childhood Arrivals (DACA) protection from deportation.

Several of these mothers could have had special protections from deportation themselves as victims of domestic abuse but did not know about the U Visa that made this possible until it was too late. They were already separated from their children by a walled-off, militarized border. In their cases, as is too often the case within the immigrant community, mediocre lawyers did not have the wherewithal to apply for the appropriate protection after detainment and before deportation.

The U Visa program allows for some measure of mercy to protect domestic abuse survivors. It's a helpful aid, in theory and when employed correctly, but many undocumented women experience domestic violence, not knowing that they could get out of the abusive situation while also finding legal status. As immigrants living in the shadows, this kind of opportunity is out of their ordinary experience and, therefore, out of their realm of knowledge. It's just another example of the broken and unjust immigration system in the US.

Tania's case is different. She was deported before DACA was the law of the land and didn't qualify for a U Visa. If her case had come up later, she would have been covered by DACA since Tania was only three years old when her family crossed from Mexico.

Tania was born in Guadalajara, Jalisco, Mexico, in 1986. When speaking to her in Guillermo's office, I mention our similar ages, and her wry wit shines when she says, "We are getting old." Her family moved to Los Angeles from Jalisco, but she doesn't even remember living in Mexico. When she was deported, L.A. was the only home she had ever known. Now, she knows Tijuana, too.

When I ask her how she ended up here, her to-the-point mentality keeps us on track as she tells me, "I got deported." She was not deported with anyone from her family, although her mom and dad also "got deported" later on. The only companions she had on this journey were her fellow deportees in a government van.

Part of why Tania got deported alone was because she was trying to keep the whereabouts of her parents a secret from the ICE agents who were questioning her. It seemed like they were going to let her go if she gave up the location of her dad, whom they had apparently been hunting for a long time—"like he was some kind of criminal," says Tania. That loyalty to her family means Tania has now spent over a decade looking out over a fence to the country and *el sueño americano* (the American dream) her parents worked so hard for their family to achieve.

Tania's heart is in L.A. That's the place she calls home more than Tijuana. Home certainly is not San Diego, just over the wall. She tells me that she has never been to San Diego, so she cannot speak directly about that side. To her, though, Tijuana seems similar to where she used to live in

Los Angeles. Each has international people, which makes them feel "pretty much the same." The area of L.A. where she grew up and spent her early adult years was not all that appealing either—a striking similarity.

The most significant difference between the two locations is that Tania does not want to live in Mexico: "I don't think I can get used to being here." This desire to leave is fundamentally rooted in family: "I have a daughter in L.A." The border and the governmental authorities enforcing it separate Tania from the person she loves most in the entire world, and her deportation has left her daughter motherless for over a decade.

As for Tijuana, it's not her home, but Tania does not have anything against it. When talking about how it has changed since her arrival, her first thought goes to deportees like herself: "Oh, woo . . . When I got deported, there wasn't someone at the door to help you." Now, though, she tells me that at least there are services at the port of entry.

Tijuana has changed since Tania's arrival, but so has she. The way she talks about it displays her inner conflict: "I don't think I've changed. I think I've gotten worse." Perhaps she notices the apparent contradiction as she clarifies: "I think I've gotten worse with my emotions and how I think." Tania's dark emotions are admittedly because of the grief that continues to haunt her. Even though she and other deportees like her have more opportunities in Tijuana now than they did when she first arrived, she cannot get over the fact that her child is back in the US. She thinks that her relatives are also unable to move past this grim reality of family separation. Regardless, she is glad that people who live in the area don't automatically think of her and other deportees as criminals.

Tania's only firsthand knowledge of San Diego is what she saw through the deportation van's windows and what she can view from the south side of its 18- and 30-foot fences. She tells me that it looks pretty from far away but that she does not really "look into it" because she is "looking into L.A." Her friends tell her San Diego is lovely. Still, it is evident from our conversation that she is fixated on her home city and on her daughter, who lives there.

The rootedness of Tania's story in L.A. becomes even more apparent to me as she continues to compare Tijuana with Los Angeles, telling me, "I don't think it's as bad as people make it seem. That's for sure," and, "If someone gets shot, it's because they're in a bad situation or they get into a bad situation." For her, Tijuana is just like L.A. Gangs, drugs, and violence exist, but you will be fine if you keep out of harm's way. She also compares how she feels in Tijuana to how she felt in Los Angeles, though one aspect of her feeling was more favorable toward Tijuana. In the US, Tania did not feel safe. She was constantly at risk of being deported, and that gave her tremendous anxiety.

Tania hadn't always been undocumented while living in the US. She had legal status starting in 1997, but then she lived without papers from 2002–2010. Like I have heard too often, it seems to have been a clerical mistake that led her on the road to illegality in the eyes of the US federal government.

She tells me it was her mom who was in charge of getting the paperwork renewed but that those who appeared to be lawyers, in actuality, were not. There is an unmistakable sense of unknowing, though, because, as she states: "I wasn't involved in the case." She also recounts the plight of living without papers and having her permission to work denied and "all this stuff." The overwhelming and all-encompassing nature of life as an undocumented immigrant in the United States cannot be more concisely expressed than in those three words: "all this stuff."

Contrasting it to her experience on the northern side of the border, Tania says, "Tijuana has accepted me" and "I can't really say anything bad about Tijuana." However, she also speaks of the hardship she experienced when she first arrived. She tells me: "It's funny how we were born here, but they have no idea who we are when we step here." She struggled for two years to convince the Mexican government that Mexico was where she was born. Her frustration is evident as she tells me that even though her birth certificate stated she was from Guadalajara, that was not enough; Tania had to bring in witnesses to show who she was. She compares it to the present day again: "There was not as much help as there is now."

Speaking of the Mexican borderlands, Tania's daily life is fully on the *frontera* of Tijuana. All of her work, school, family, and activist endeavors find their home here, even as her heart seeks to be elsewhere. Her mom and dad live with her again since they were deported not too long after Tania was. Beyond that, she has other relatives nearby, but they are close in proximity only.

"They tell me to make a life here," says Tania, but she feels as though this would mean forsaking her daughter in California. Because of this conflict, Tania tells me, "I stay away from my family."

As we both sip coffee hand-delivered by our mutual friend Guillermo, Tania tells me more about her family with a focus on her daughter. Years back, they used to converse via Skype, but they lost contact from 2016 to 2018 before reconnecting over FaceTime. The only reason Tania has been able to speak with her recently is that her daughter's father has reopened the custody battle against Tania and is trying to strip her of custody rights. Tania never goes into her past or present relationship with him, but I cannot imagine it is a healthy one if he is trying to take away her parental rights. Tania has a US lawyer who is helping, but she receives little help from Mexican authorities. She tells me, "No one really cares on this side." She also describes how she gets judged in Tijuana as people ask, "Why didn't you *bring* her?"

Like any deportee cut off from home, Tania has to make a living. She is trying to become a cosmetology instructor through an online school. Tania was a cosmetologist in the US after graduating from high school since her undocumented status barred her from attending a "big university." She has also studied "advanced computers," but she isn't working in tech right now.

Until she finishes school, Tania will probably continue her employment in the accounting department at an American t-shirt company. She works Monday through Friday, ten hours a day. Sometimes, Tania works on Saturdays too. Her co-workers are from all over, and they speak Spanish, English, or both.

Tania explains how Tijuana residents say, "You're taking our jobs." I find myself struck by how this is not so dissimilar to the rhetoric on my side of the fence. She continues: "We are like trash to them, but we are taking their jobs from them." Tania does not appreciate how some people act toward her because of her Angeleno Spanish accent and because she is "always talking English." For Tania, her first language is always going to be English, and she tells me, "I feel better when I speak English." That reality seems to make her work life more palatable because she uses a lot of English in her job at an American corporation.

Speaking of language, on the day of our interview, I break down the strict interviewer-interviewee construct intentionally as we discuss the bilingual household. Tania expresses that her use of Spanglish and English in her home often leads to arguments between her and her mom: "My mom hates me when I do that." Tania's response is always: "You raised me in the US" or "It's good to know both." I know from other families, including my own, that disagreements regarding language are a source of ongoing tension in immigrant homes.

After our cathartic moment sharing in the frustrations of family and the hopes for more language inclusivity, she tells me that English is more highly regarded in Tijuana than it was in the past because it provides access to certain economic benefits. Even though Tania makes more money as a bilingual person than she would otherwise, she confesses that she still does not like American-owned, Mexican-operated *maquiladoras*.[8] She also shares her opinion that most people in Tijuana are solely focused on their daily cooking, cleaning, and other tasks. She seems to think this leads to complacency, which gets in the way of folks in Tijuana succeeding or finding greater possibilities. However, she finds that some eventually start seeing the benefits the US companies bring.

Outside of school, work, and family life, Tania is also dedicated to using her experience to help the people of the *frontera*. She consistently shares with others the help that she needed upon arrival to Mexico. For those who find themselves displaced in Tijuana, she gives "feedback with what I went through." Her lived experience becomes a source of practical wisdom for newcomers. She also makes sure to focus on herself from time to time to "get all of those bad ideas out" and focus on the good.

Tania returns to the theme of motherhood here as she tells me that even though she has a life in Tijuana, it is challenging emotionally. Being without her daughter is the chief contributing factor to her emotional trauma: "It kills me."

Channeling her emotion into creativity, Tania has "a really, really big goal—to help childhood arrivals like myself." If something terrible were to happen to them, she believes, they would end up in the same situation as her. "I see a bunch of youngsters doing drugs and prostituting." She cannot stomach this, so she has started the DREAM

Will project. The end goal is to have what she calls a Dream Center to help with education "as much as we can." I ask if it is primarily for deportees, but her vision is to reach an even broader mix of people. She tells me it is for anyone who has a dream to do something: "computer information, education, documentation, classes of any sort."

She sees US and Mexican laws as the impediment to her ultimate vision of helping people. She is not specific, but I assume she is speaking about unjust laws related to the border and immigration and education and social services. From her vantage point and mine, US immigration law as it exists today is deeply flawed.

Our conversation turns to the Border Church. Tania's faith is as simple as it is rooted. She says, "Wherever God is, that's religion." Tania is Catholic but not tied to that label, in part because she considers herself Christian "in general." Though some kinds of events, like weddings, remind her of her former Catholic practice while in Los Angeles, her thinking has since expanded, which is apparent when she now lumps together "Catholic, Muslim, whatever." Her idea of the *basileia* is more open than my fundamentalist-formed ecclesiastical impulses.

Yet, her "whatever" approach is part and parcel of a *fronteriza* faith. Tania is more interested in the practice of faith than organizational affiliation, doctrinal fidelity, or adherence to institutional codes. She tells me that what she knows about God is what we have to practice for ourselves, citing one poignant example: "Take your jacket off and give it to others." She tries to live by this principle of faithful service.

The theme of helping even frames her description of the Border Church. Tania says that when the congregation meets each Sunday, there are always ways to contribute. I can tell that in her way of thinking, the contribution is not merely a worship ritual or offering; instead, it is a direct contribution to those in need who come from all over Tijuana to receive services on Sundays.

As much as she liked going to the Catholic church she attended while growing up, she describes how the Border Church is a little different since there is always help available. "At regular church, you just go and do." Tania contrasts this with the Border Church, where you do not have to wait in line to confess your sins to the priest. She takes it a step further, too, when she says, "There's no need to confess [because] we are all in the same situation." I am left wondering what group confession and pardon mean to her and to others who were raised in the Latin-American Catholic Church and taught the importance of penance.

Tania continues to demonstrate her non-institutional ways of thinking when she says that connection with churches and denominations does matter because many people worldwide come through them. Moreover, she sees a spiritual connection in these partnerships. For Tania, "it works well spiritually."

Closer to home, Tania describes how everyone at the Border Church "is pretty much in the same situation as myself. I feel like I'm in my community." People have told Tania their stories, and she knows that they can relate because they have experienced many of the same issues. She originally came to the Border Church in 2013 simply because she was at the border trying to pick up US cell phone service: "That's how I got to know people. That's how I got into groups. I used to just stand there looking for signal." In a similar manner to how she came to Friendship Park looking for connection, she knows that others come to this area of Playas every day searching for things they need. Many of the people here need some form of assistance, and they often ask what the Border Church is and how it can help them.

When I inquire about the specific elements of worship, Tania's answer surprises me. It is not from the list of practices I bring up. It is not even directly related to the Border

Church. For Tania, "the more meaningful one is when they open the doors. It gives people hope by seeing or touching. People always want to interact and want that closure. Whatever we do there, it's never going to be cute or nice emotionally because they want closure."

Tania always tells me she likes seeing Pastor John and that she knows I am on the US side frequently now. She continues to talk about how, besides all of the festivals and rituals people do as a church, people need spiritual help too. "And people need food." She again confirms that the door in the border fence opening up is what she appreciates most and that the church is "number two." When Tania sees through that door to the other side, even though the last time that happened was in 2016, she feels some hope. Though there's that hope at the Border Church, "even sometimes the spiritual stuff doesn't help me out. There needs to be something physical."

Nevertheless, the church's spiritual work has meaning for her, and it seems that the spiritual community gives her the most meaning. Tania tells me that being in a community with other deportees gives her "that type of closure" she needs. She goes on to say that the closure is not final: "Unfortunately, it helps with the pain just when we're there. I don't want to say it, but that's how it is. I think it's good because you have this Saturday and Sunday to start again. But for us, we have to go back into it. But it's good. It gives you hope." That fleeting hope, as we will discuss later, is a window into God's *basileia*.

The hope for the future that Tania has is light. She hopes that people can come to the Border Church and be in a building or at least someplace where people can interact with and touch each other. For her, even a detention center, where you can sit across from loved ones and talk, would be a win. That is a short-term hope for Tania, and her medium-range aspiration is even greater. She states it this way: "Oh, if you guys could tear that damn wall down, that would be, yeah." Beyond that, Tania has long-term hope for different laws that would change the situation so radically that "there would be no need for us to be there." She sees this as a challenging goal to achieve, but she still hopes that it will one day become a reality. She simply wants moms to be able to be with their children.

As we end the formal interview, and just before she decides to put off schoolwork to help our friend Guillermo with a visit to the canyons where some migrants live, she tells me that the Border Church has always supported her in whatever situation she was in.

A few minutes later, I walk back toward the border and wave to the two of them as they embody the Border Church's ethos and engage in a spirited and caring conversation with a wheelchair-bound man who, like many marginalized individuals in Tijuana, sells candy to eke out a living. Tania has been supported, yes. Yet, I find it evident that she also acts on behalf of others as an integral member of the Border Church.

Tania's story is one of a mother whose love is reaching beyond her capacity. As a deportee, she cannot legally travel to L.A. to see her daughter and cannot return to the City of Angels that her heart calls home without finding grave repercussions there. Yet, her love is not useless where she does have the space to employ it—here on the borderlands. With Tania in mind, not merely as an object of study but as a subject I regard highly, let us consider three segments of theological gifts we can receive from Tania's experience: identity, innocence, and *agape*.

Identity

From a theological perspective, Tania's is interesting. Her identities lie outside of neat categories and boxes. She's an Angelena but cannot even visit L.A., much less live there, at least not until she gets the proper documentation. Tania's story begs the question: What is identity? And what does it have to do with God?

The love of place is at the heart of Tania's identity as an Angelena. L.A. is her home. More than that, the people there are her people. She feels out of place when people put down her non-*Tijuanense* accent or dismiss her English skills. She feels at home in L.A. because it is full of people like her. Not unlike the displaced Hebrew people in ancient Babylon or so many modern diaspora communities, Tania's neighbors came from elsewhere. Tania was used to being around groups of people who have Latin American roots and culture but come together as Angelenos. Calling L.A. home defines them perhaps as much as their personal and family backgrounds.

I was happily surprised that during his inaugural address, President Joseph R. Biden channeled Augustine of Hippo when he claimed that "a people is a multitude of rational beings joined together by common agreement on the objects of their love."[7] More simply, a people is defined by its shared love. When the president said this, especially only two weeks after a violent insurrection and storming of the capitol building left five people dead and more than one hundred injured, I wondered if the citizens of the United States have enough of a shared love to even be called "the American people."

I still wonder. But as I think about Tania, I know that she and many of her fellow Angelenos love that city and what it stands for—a place where people from all backgrounds and walks of life can live side by side. A huge hindrance to making this idealistic vision a reality is a legal system that basically says, "If you weren't born here, you don't belong here." In many cases, people who experience daily discrimination are still treated like they don't belong, even if they *were* born here in the US. In doing so, our so-called Christian nation disregards the love St. Augustine espoused and the call to love on the part of that old saint's Savior.

Defining what a people holds as a shared object of love is a challenging, perhaps impossible, task, especially as the modern movement of peoples worldwide continues to accelerate, mixing up the relative homogeneity of past epochs. The borderlands are chock-full of cross-cutting identities and, as such, serve as a prime example of this challenge. Regardless, whether it's a combination of a place, ideas, or self-descriptions, a people can and will share a measure of common values and identities.

As members of the divine *basileia*, we need not allow our identities to separate us from the ultimate object of love, namely Jesus. And more than an object of some esoteric system or depersonalized set of rules, Jesus is a subject who loves us back. Too often, in our increasingly polarized society, we let our perceived differences in identity get in the way of good relationships in the church instead of making room for the *basileia* in our midst (Luke 17:21).

The multiple identities we have within this nation are starting to merge into two large groups and to cause a huge rift. Lilliana Mason argues in *Uncivil Agreement: How Politics Became Our Identity* that the two major political parties in the United States are now rooted in mega-identities coalescing around social factors.[9] As that happens, it can make the other "side" seem like pure evil. More and more, people are leaving the church because they feel like they do not and cannot fit within it. I know for a fact that some of my political opinions make people from previous chapters of my life, namely those whose evangelical background shapes their understanding of Christianity, skeptical of my discipleship as a follower of Jesus. Reading the pages of this book may only confirm for some that I have moved outside of "legitimate" Christianity.

Regardless, I realize that the idea of Christian identity, especially in its contemporary white nationalist flavor, can be used against people of other faiths or of no faith. What I am advocating for is not using our Christian identity as a bludgeon in the culture wars. Instead, let's utilize it to build community among ourselves. Christ—I hope—is our shared love. If so, he's what holds us together as a people. It is from this place that we can and should seek the kind of justice that the *basileia* deserves, demands, and delivers.

Christ loved us enough to call us friends and siblings. It's this Divine One who took on flesh to dwell among us. It's this Anointed One whom we serve as our King and Lord. It's this Jesus who is the human face of God. All humans stand equal before Jesus and can find our identity in being the beloved children of God just like their brother Jesus. I hope this brief discussion of identity in Christ will cause you to reflect on which aspects of your identity matter most to you. I also hope you're encouraged to use each aspect of your identity for the benefit of yourself and your neighbors.

Innocence

It's relatively easy to be sympathetic toward a person like Tania, who got caught up in the thick of immigration policy by no fault of her own. Tania was three years old when she arrived in the US. The lawyers her parents hired were frauds. She chose not to rat out her dad out of fear of what ICE would do to him. True, some people may fault her for getting caught. She did, after all, have a loud fight with a friend—the same friend who later met her in Tijuana to help her get back on her feet—which resulted in the arrival of police and ICE. Regardless, she is one of the "innocent ones."

When thinking about the immigrant population, it may be easier to consider these innocent ones as worthier of grace than those who are convicted of more serious crimes. But for me, breaking an unjust law cannot make the offender guilty in any absolute sense. If I opened my Bible, I'd contend for immigrants' rights from the overwhelming number and clarity of its passages—including Deuteronomy 10:19, Leviticus 19:34 and 27:19, 1 Chronicles 16:19-22, Psalm 146:9, Jeremiah 7:5-7, Ezra 47:22, Zechariah 7:9-10, Matthew 25:35, Luke 10:25-37, Romans 12:13, and Hebrews 13:1-3, among others—all of which demonstrate that the ancient followers of the God of Abraham, Isaac, and Jacob must follow God by welcoming strangers, foreigners, and misfits. The leap from interpretation to application should not be difficult. We need to live according to a divinely loving principle of welcome as members of the *basileia*.

As for the concepts of innocence and guilt, I've told my therapist how my fundamentalist upbringing has left me with certain verses that haunt me. One that really sticks with me is Romans 3:23, which reminds us that all of us have sinned and that we all fall short. While I do not deny the truth of this statement, I prefer not to dwell on everyone's shortcomings. Why not? Because I find that most people are already aware that they are flawed and sinful.

I acknowledge that nobody is entirely innocent. Individuals do have personal responsibility for their actions. One's ability to be responsible is impacted dramatically by sociocultural, historical, and familial context, but it still exists. To perceive everyone as completely innocent is to be out of touch with reality. But we can move beyond these notions of innocence and guilt when it comes to welcoming our neighbors. To welcome is not to judge someone as "good" or "bad." All you have to do is say, "You're here," and "I accept you." Love does not deny or ignore guilt or innocence, but it follows the Christ, whose radical welcome included those deemed guilty in the eyes of society. This is the same Christ whose life is an example of true innocence, yet he did not use his perfection to gain power or to make others feel bad about themselves. Jesus is the pinnacle of real love. Many of us jump too quickly to moral judgments that parrot the political right or left more than striving for the love that Jesus exemplifies.

Agape

Speaking of Jesus' love, one of my favorite images in the Gospels is when Jesus describes himself as a chicken. Seriously, a chicken. Can you picture it? The Savior of all describes himself as a chicken.

Jesus likens himself to a chicken to show his love. Specifically, in Luke 13:34-35, Jesus laments to Jerusalem that he has often wanted to gather the city's people in the same way that a mother hen gathers her chicks under her wings. Yet, Jerusalem refused to obey God's commands. So, Jesus let Jerusalem's chickens come home to roost.

"Jesus the mother" is not a concept that is especially popular within mainstream Christianity. There's a cult here or there in addition to some progressive theologians who take the deep dive into the femininity of Jesus. Yet, in mainstream Christianity, Jesus is conceived of in mostly masculine terms. He was a man in a literal sense, so this is not entirely unwarranted. But as God, the divine nature of the Human One incorporates and transcends any gender identity. Within that transcendent space, we can understand Jesus as more than just a man. Indeed, we must conceive of Jesus as a mother.

Jesus, the mother who beckons the children of Jerusalem to come home, is not unlike Tania. These moms are separated from their offspring. A critical difference from the chicks of Jerusalem is that Tania's now-teenage daughter did not choose to be kept away from her mom as a little girl. The government and Tania's ex decided to keep this mother-daughter duo apart. How much the Divine Mother must long for this separation to end in a heartfelt homecoming.

As *madres*, both Jesus and Tania have been ridiculed for not doing more to get their children back. Yet, they both have used motherly discretion in not violating the rights of their children. Similarly, Jesus didn't want to infringe upon the free will of the Jerusalemites. Tania does not want to remove her daughter from her rights as an American citizen living in the place Tania still considers home and knows is her daughter's home, too.

There are, of course, more differences between Tania and Jesus. Nevertheless, when I think about the struggles of family separation that too many moms, dads, and other loved ones undergo at the border, I cannot help but think about Jesus' little chicks separated from him. In certain spiritualities, such as that of Ignatius of Loyola, reading the scriptures serves as an invitation for us to see ourselves and our communities in the stories of the Bible. That's how I see my friend Tania in this Gospel passage. Yet, there are many more separated families that we could see in the text as well. They may be separated because of willfulness on the part of one or more family members, or perhaps due to systems of oppression surrounding the southern border of the US. Whatever the particular reasons are, there is a measure of suffering that cannot be denied.

Jesus lamented like a hen for her chicks. Jesus, as a mother, wanted so badly to be with her family. Families separated because of economic and political realities should have the right to lament in public just like Jesus did. There should be space in our churches to stop pretending that everything is fine and to be real so that we can weep with others when they weep. We, too, should be able to lament the injustice in this world that makes Tania's situation and the hardships of those in similar circumstances all too common in our broken world. Our lament must move beyond self-pity and guilt into care and action to help ease the world's pain.

We are invited to use whatever privilege and authority we have to work on behalf of justice for those separated from their families. Part of the worldwide church has been on a mission for a long time to stop these inhumane family separations. It's high time to address the grief of separated parents and their children.

The Border Church is doing this work of bringing people together in love. It is not set up as a legal service to unite Tania and her daughter. We have neither the resources nor the expertise to do that. What we do have is the love of Christ. Tania herself knows what it's like to feel the relief of coming to the communion table and the lunch table for fellowship, camaraderie, and unity. Coming to this church does not fix her problems or catapult her over the wall, but it offers momentary hope that something good is happening and that something better is coming. There's a communion of love she can tap into, as well as a people centered on the love of Christ. Even though they can never replace her daughter, they can give and receive a knowing love.

May all of our congregations be so loving.

NOTES

1. "The Kumeyaay of Southern California," http://www.kumeyaay.info/kumeyaay/.
2. "Treaty of Guadalupe Hidalgo," *Encyclopedia Britannica*, https://www.britannica.com/event/Treaty-of-Guadalupe-Hidalgo.
3. Wikipedia, "Transborder Agglomeration," February 11, 2021, https://en.wikipedia.org/wiki/Transborder_agglomeration.
4. Barbara Zaragoza, *San Ysidro and the Tijuana River Valley*, Images of America (Charleston, SC: Arcadia, 2014), 23–24.
5. Katharina Buccholz, "Turnaround for US Deportations under Biden?" *Stastica*, February 11, 2021, https://www.statista.com/

chart/18162/deportations-and-returns-in-the-us-foreigners
-immigration/.

6. Migration Policy Institute, "Major US Immigration Laws, 1790–
    Present," 2013, https://www.migrationpolicy.org/sites/default/files/
    publications/CIR-1790Timeline.pdf; Southern Border Communities
    Coalition, "Operation Gatekeeper and the Birth of Border
    Militarization," 2019, https://www.southernborder.org/operation
    _gatekeeper; Cheyenne Haslett, "Trump Declares National
    Emergency to Get Border Wall Funding," February 15, 2019, ABC
    News, https://abcnews.go.com/Politics/trump-sign-border
    -bill-declare-national-emergency-wall/story?id=61088949.

7. Adam Rasmussen, "Joe Biden Quotes St. Augustine: Context."
    Where Peter Is, January 20, 2021, https://wherepeteris.com/joe-biden
    -quotes-st-augustine-context/.

8. A company that allows factories to be largely duty free and
    tariff-free.

9. Lilliana Mason, *Uncivil Agreement: How Politics Became Our
    Identity* (Chicago: University of Chicago Press, 2018).

AN ACCOMPANYING TOUR GUIDE

Guillermo Navarrete is the lay pastor on the Mexican side of our one-wall church. His daily life, more than that of any other person on earth, is dedicated to the unique work of this particular congregation and the variety of ministry opportunities it affords at and near the border.

Guillermo was born in Tampico, Mexico, a city on the Gulf Coast. He lived there for the first eighteen years of his life before entering university and joining the Mexican Merchant Marines as a naval mechanical engineer in service of Petróleos Mexicanos (Pemex), Mexico's federally owned petroleum company. Guillermo tells me, "I lived on the ocean. I still have salt in my veins," while thumping the skin over the blood vessels of his arm. As a communicator, Guillermo is very charismatic both in his speech and in his expressive body language. Every time he says something, Guillermo employs a kind of embodied gesture that is both thoroughly Mexican and entirely his own.

As much as he loved the sea, Guillermo saw how being on ships for months at a time disrupted the family lives of his fellow seamen. They only saw their families two or three times a year, and this was not what Guillermo wanted for himself once he had a family. So, eventually, he left the waters he loved and moved in with his mother's relatives on the dry land of Tijuana. One year later, the family he was born into moved from Tampico to join him and, eventually, the rest of his own family.

Guillermo tells me about the impact the border has on the region he now calls home, including the personal impact of an expiring visa when he did not have the money to renew it. Because of his previously defunct documentation, he spent eleven years unable to cross the border. He thanks God that he received his visa again in 2019, especially since a visa is indispensable for the Border Church's binational work. Guillermo is happy to now have the privilege to cross, and he believes his experience helped him understand what Tijuana is like apart from San Diego.

As an engineer, Guillermo is always categorizing things. For him, three types of borderland people make their way in the region. One is a *Tijuanense* who cannot cross, another is a *Tijuanense* who can and does cross, and the final is a US citizen who can cross freely. The inequality seen in these three groups is palpable and heartbreaking.

Though the word may ring harsh in certain contexts, Guillermo is apt to discuss the "obligations" of Tijuana and San Diego residents, "all people have rights, by virtue of the fulfillment of the obligations, as a resident of any city, state, or country." It is through meeting these obligations that people earn their rights; there are two sides to one coin. I am not completely sure if he means this in a practical or a philosophical sense, but either way, fulfilling duties for one's place of residence is of utmost importance to Guillermo.

One thing I love about Guillermo, even if it embarrasses me more than I wish, is that he is chock-full of hot takes. With enthusiasm and a slight sense of begrudging, Guillermo has more than once proclaimed about San Diego and

Tijuana: "You *take* the valleys, and you *leave* us the hills!" The present tense of the utterance displays the ongoing reality of past national action.

As for his own four-plus decades in this part of what's still Mexico, Guillermo recounts the changes that have occurred in Tijuana. He fondly tells of his early days in the city when a person could safely leave their bicycle outside their home and leave the front door unlocked. This is no longer a reality; Guillermo explains that nowadays, if you leave your bike outside for even a moment, the next time you'll see it will be at the recycling plant—in pieces.

In our conversations, Guillermo leads us back to obligations and how many people in Tijuana can't meet them. He also discusses how many people live in the area without legal residency and how he views that as a critical social problem. He says of undocumented people living in Mexico: "Without personal identification documents, [they] roam the streets in search of opportunities that, without social support, divert their good intentions and take actions against the good living of society." He believes this societal crisis started about twenty years ago. Before then, migrants came alone or in small groups, but now they come in "a long line," causing social problems.

Part of the problem, as he sees it, stems from binational border enforcement policies. Guillermo remembers forty years ago when the border was effectively open. Since then, however, "they enforce more and more." After the terrorist attacks of September 11, 2001, and the creation of the department of Homeland Security, the way the US has attended to the border has caused an increasingly devastating "social problem" on the Mexican side. Guillermo and I both see the lack of justice from our different sides, and our hearts break over it together.

Guillermo then speaks about personal responsibility, contrary to how it is often described. Because the migrants aren't officially residents and therefore can't meet their responsibilities to the government, the government does not recognize them. Describing the situation of the homeless people, he says, "On a daily basis, the police take [people] into custody for about seventy-two hours, to investigate them. Finding nothing, they are released back out onto the street." Guillermo has also told me that in Tijuana, homeless people have two rights: the right to medical care if wounded on the streets and the right of their body to be picked up by a coroner when they die. He is not speaking of legal rights per se but of the grim realities of these marginalized people receiving the barest of medical and mortuary care as they live and die.

After bringing the conversation back to the generalities of regional change and its relation to human trafficking, organized crime, and jumping the wall, Guillermo and I discuss some personal changes he has experienced since coming to Tijuana. Always the engineer, Guillermo dissects his life into various segments. The first segment was in his family life. He was glad to have a wife and two kids, but the family-oriented utopia he thought would greet him when he came off the ships floated off more quickly than his ships ever did. The second segment was his call to mission and ministry. While studying missions in seminary, he realized, "I feel in my heart to work in Tijuana, not in Timbuktu." The truth is that there is much to be done all over the world, but because it is not the job of the Christian West to change the world, the "here" is just as good of a field for mission as the "there." More than that, "Timbuktu" is coming to Guillermo's doorstep right here in Tijuana. Migrants from both hemispheres make their way to Baja California in hopes of moving northward from there to a better life.

After Guillermo's heart was moved by the injustices he witnessed, he began working in local congregations. Yet, he was unhappy with the internally focused, "implosive" work and stagnant growth models of the churches he worked with. This eternally inward focus of local churches was exhausting for him.

Instead, he wanted to leave brick-and-mortar buildings to aid others in an "explosive" way. His third era of life in Tijuana started nearly a decade ago when Pastor John's missionary friends began coming down to Tijuana for communion at the wall. Guillermo found himself invited not merely to attend a church service but also to pick up and drive people from out of town to see what was going on at the border.

What he witnessed opened his heart and mind: "It was a shocking thing to learn what migration was all about, and we ended [up] at El Faro" for a church service. There, he found a company of people who had a keen desire to meet the physical and spiritual needs of displaced persons impacted by migration patterns and immigration laws. Essentially, the Border Church has a community of people who want to accompany anyone in need of "bread" along the way.

Guillermo grew up Presbyterian and now is a Methodist. Having such a background in the Protestant faith, he tells me that it is impossible to describe Christianity in brief, though he tries, saying: "Do the will [of God]. That's it, and the church is not doing it." Guillermo goes further in describing how a typical church only grows "implosively." By that, he means it is navel-gazing. Few people in typical churches look to the streets to see what God is doing and how to take part; the people only care about themselves and what happens inside the church walls.

Guillermo thinks God leads people into the church, but he only sees models he describes as "recycling, recycling, recycling." The recycled leaders lead, according to Guillermo, too many other leaders with too many thoughts. Since there is not more to do, he thinks these leaders just fight one another, which eventually leads to division. He reminds me that God does not divide but instead multiplies, while people cause division instead of getting outside to multiply their efforts.

Guillermo contrasts the example of the divisive and internally focused church with the Border Church. He tells me, "Let's start at the bottom. The bottom for me is Jesus." What does that mean? For Guillermo, it means that Jesus only went to the temple three or four times during his three years of earthly ministry. So, where was Jesus? Guillermo says he was on the roads, on the hillsides, and at the beach; he was with the people. Guillermo sees his appointment as one that is outside with the migrants. Here, he can simply ask people if they are migrants and figure out how he can accompany them.

The English word *accompany* and its Spanish cognate *acompañar* originally come from late Latin (the English version by way of French).[1] In Latin, like in Spanish, the prefix *a* means "to" or "toward." What English held onto in words such as *accompanist*, *company*, and *companion* was *com*. Spanish has the similar *con* as both a standalone preposition and a prefix meaning "with." Finally, the Latin *panis* and its shortened Spanish descendent *pan* both mean "bread." This is not how a language professor would describe the term, but to accompany/*acompañar* someone has a real sense of sharing bread with them.

As such, when we accompany/*acompañamos* a person or group, we are sharing "bread" with them. This is such a fitting understanding for what Guillermo and his companions at the Border Church do in a physical and spiritual sense. It's an essential part of the *basileia* spirit.

In a recent discussion with Guillermo, he mentions that early on, he started noticing the harsh living conditions that many who called Tijuana their temporary home had to survive. Before then, he was focused on his own problems and chose to ignore their plight, but after a while, he could no longer ignore them.

More than any other person I interviewed for this book, Guillermo always wants to steer our discussion toward the work of the Border Church, but he doesn't mind when I ask him to zoom out and focus on the broader system. We talk about the ever-changing and seemingly ever-growing economies of San Diego and Tijuana, in addition to the relative lack of political change and progress for the most marginalized.

Guillermo raises his hands high as he talks about our two nations' presidents meeting each other in a lofty manner, far removed from the people. He lowers them as he brings the conversation back down to the people directly impacted by border policies. These leaders dole out laws to which the populations reply: "Hey, why you not ask me?" From Guillermo's perspective, one political reality that has been true for the last twenty-five years is that of separated families due to deportations. Countless young people lack one or both parents, causing many of them to distrust the government. He thinks that fragmented families are dysfunctional families.

We shift our conversation from families to food, a topic near and dear to Guillermo. He boasts about the great culinary scene that Tijuana has and how it is better than that of San Diego. The bustling food scene is what he likes most about the region. What he likes least is the "human situation on both sides." Migration, deportation, and homelessness are crises that impact both sides of this vast metropolitan region. Shocking to the migrants are the homeless Americans who travel down to Tijuana, as well as nearly Rosarito and Ensenada, and beg on the streets. "Why is the gringo here?" they ask Guillermo. He informs them that most of these US-born street dwellers are addicted to drugs.

Guillermo's daily life is full. Until his son's recent wedding, both of his adult children lived with him and his wife, who happens to call him while we are discussing family life. Though his dreams of spending ample time with his family did not ultimately pan out, it is apparent that he is proud of his children, who are musicians. Just like when they were growing up, Guillermo's days are filled with work. He does Border Church work Sunday through Friday and takes Saturday off to rest. He also works in the morning at a nonprofit kitchen that cooks for the *maquiladoras* and is trying to grow. Guillermo tells me he has "good work skills in management," in part because he has been a manager in every job he has had since his role as a technician.

I sense the friction that exists between his managerial ways and the deeper desires of his heart for union with God while working toward God's justice and *basileia*. Guillermo expresses that his favorite part of the work is being "with the people" and that his least favorite part is dealing with "administration." It is taxing to try to keep everything orderly with all that is going on, including the frequent changes in migration patterns and the amorphous nature of immigration policies on either side of the fence.

Guillermo tells me about his desire to be with the people on Sundays so that he can care for them, as well as his desire to set up a team that can carry out the logistical work of setting up an outdoor church service. Guillermo admits he is a workaholic who prefers to sit in front of the computer doing more work even after hours. He tells me of his many "hats" and how he needs to give them away. My friend is happy that the team at El Faro has taken some of those logistics hats away from him. Knowing this, Guillermo is trying to work himself out of many jobs to focus on accompanying the people.

Guillermo wants to maintain his health in order to continue doing this work because he is, in his words, "old." He calculates that he only has 15 percent of his life left based on a scale of eighty years. Of all the spiritual realities and

Christian teachings circulating in his mind, what Guillermo senses as the most crucial concept to live out is obedience to God. He says that we need to be in touch with God so that we can follow God, and he believes he has unnecessary problems because of all his hats. Guillermo feels a profound need to teach the people to do the work of focusing on God's will.

Guillermo shares his favorite example of obedience to God: a meditation experience in which he felt both his own spirit and the Holy Spirit within his body. With his eyes closed, his arms stretched forward, and his face "burning," Guillermo felt heat coming through his palm, so he opened his eyes to see what was going on. Just then, the man who was right in front of him fell on the floor. Guillermo grabbed his hat and coat and ran to the corner, asking, "What was that?" In telling this story, Guillermo explains that his main takeaway from the situation was not the fact that the man collapsed; it was that he could feel God doing something within him.

Similarly, when he meditates with friends, he can feel his spirit—not his thoughts, feelings, or will, which become silent. It is not even the Holy Spirit, but the human spirit, that he feels. This worship from one's spirit, he thinks, is what it means to worship "in spirit and in truth," like in John 4:24. He says, "My spirit is the holy-holy place, where Jesus makes the throne in your life." Guillermo wants to focus his energy on his spiritual holiness in the final fraction of his time on earth, so he pursues obedience through consistent morning prayer. In this shift, his desire is to seek God's *basileia* now.

Guillermo likes to reflect on our faith embodied at the wall. He has told me, "At the Border Church, my leader is Jesus." Guillermo sees how Border Church members are in the streets just like Jesus was. He notes, "When someone comes, they'll see the truth." The truth for him is going outside of the church to help vulnerable people, including migrants and deportees. Guillermo's work, as I see it, is a prime example of how the borderlands can start to look just ever so slightly more like heaven as the *basileia* shows itself in glimpses.

Guillermo senses the need for an externally facing church when he talks about the partnerships needed to make Border Church work. More than merely associating with churches and denominations, Guillermo tells me that he continues to work with the government, the police, and many Tijuana-based neighborhood councils. He also goes outside of Christianity's typical boundaries to talk about the involvement of people from non-Christian faiths.

We discuss the logistics of the Sunday service. In the past, his Sundays—and home—were a mess. Now, "it's easy." He walks me through his typical Sunday, which is consistent with what others have described aside from some minute personal details. He tells me that he is the lay pastor, but he has handed off the coordinating job to his companion Robert.

As we continue to think about the Border Church's Sunday service, I ask Guillermo what is the most essential element to him. He tells me that for him, the confession, pardon, and forgiveness prayer and communion are the best parts. Guillermo immediately explains that because individuals cannot be there every week, we need to allow them to receive the support they need directly from God. That support is found in confession, pardon, and partaking in communion. Guillermo posits how we must come to the wall for confession and share energy through the border. There is power there. He also feels the presence of God there because he sees the changes in people's faces when pardon is offered. Some look as though they are in shock. Others look elated. He sees this transformation whenever people participate in communion.

Guillermo sums up the work we do and the acts of worship we perform at the Border Church as doing "the will of God," his key practice for Christian life. To him, each Sunday is different because different people come every week. The ambiance changes. Sometimes, there are many tears, like when a man hired a trio to sing through the fence to the wife he cannot embrace. Other times, the atmosphere is tense, such as when Guillermo's deported friend had a cold interaction with a suited-up American who turned out to be a lawyer serving divorce papers. Even in those challenging situations, there is an overarching sense of solidarity on the Mexican side of the fence.

Guillermo says less about the joyful ambiance at the borderline of Friendship Park. Instead, he moves on to answer my question about the Border Church's impact on the borderlands regions. He starts with a statement that is perhaps as profound as it is obvious: "We are not a normal church." Guillermo clarifies by saying that we cannot measure how many people are there every Sunday, nor can we quantify to what extent people are receiving the Word of God. We do the work; we offer the communion of God through us. Then, we let God do the rest of the work. Even before anyone arrived, God was preparing them to be at the Border Church. It's not in our power. Guillermo continues to speak on the limited nature of what we can do: "We have just thirty minutes, or an hour, or two—fifty-two times a year." He finishes: "They do not depend on us but on God."

Guillermo has in the past told me about the church bus he drives, which came from John's former church: "We need a driver because I need to do the things that God is telling me to do." Guillermo loves driving. It is how he ended up at the Border Church in the first place, and it's what he wants to do when he retires from ministry. As much as Guillermo loves driving, however, he makes clear that his biggest hope and goal is simply to do God's will. For him,

that means to serve the people directly—something Guillermo senses he must do to remain obedient to God.

Accompaniment is a vital part of that obedience for
Guillermo. His heart is with the homeless migrants and
deportees first and foremost. For him, accompaniment
means holding them, listening to them, and learning from
them. Guillermo does not seem to have the savior complex
so embedded in the culture of earlier Protestant mission
work. He is not a "savior" but a person ready to walk
alongside vulnerable people. Guillermo hopes to offer hu-
manitarian help, counseling, job opportunities, and hous-
ing through mobilizing resources. Yet, he knows that the
most important thing is not merely counting numbers and
checking boxes. Of greater importance is truly being with
the people.

Some Christian thinkers, such as Richard Rohr, speak
of "reality as communion,"[2] in part based on Paul's declaration in Acts 17:28 that we "live and move and have
our being" in God. Another motif of Guillermo's accompaniment echoed in the more contemplative strain of
Christianity today is the concept of "withness." This is the
theological idea that we are united in a common union with
God and with all beings. As happens in other contexts, the
communion we at the Border Church share with God and
with one another lays the foundation for acts of accompaniment. Accompaniment is coming together in union—
communion—through time. Our borderlands work centers
on the practice of weekly communion. This sense of the
interconnectivity of all things can provide an acute and pervasive connection between the Sunday Holy Communion
event and the ongoing communion event that occurs with
every bus ride or dialogue.

What does it mean to be a tour guide? With the Bor-
der Church, it means taking people from place to place in
Tijuana. It also takes skills to inform those in one's care.
Moreover, it means caring for and traveling with those same

people. The people Guillermo drives around are primarily migrants and visiting groups from the US and Canada.

If we can take our imaginative tour together, let's do so. We're going to Practical Theology Town—a place I hope you love as much as I do. If someone who is doing ministry or justice work is a tour guide, let us consider what such a person must know and do.

Before we depart on our trip, I am aware that the concept of a tour guide may not sit well with some, especially in justice-oriented communities. How could we talk about tours without judgment when that money could be used for a better purpose? I agree, in part. Lots of tours are a complete waste of money. Beyond that, I hope you're putting your time and money where your critique is. God knows I try. If a tour and its guide aren't your jam, by all means, tweak the metaphor to one that is more appropriate to your sensibilities and context. I choose it because of the gregarious, bus-driving pastor who so often leads people to all of the right places and opens their eyes and hearts along the way.

So, here we go. What is it a tour guide must do? Tour guides have to know the purpose of the tour, know the sights, know the road, and know the tourists.

Knowing the Purpose

First and foremost, the purpose of any tour guide is to accompany the tourists on their tour. There may be a snippet in a brochure from the lobby or found at the tour company's website to describe what the tour is about. That statement of purpose needs to come alive in the knowledge, insight, and engaging delivery of the tour guide. The tour guide has to know the purpose in order to properly accompany the tourists.

In the work of justice—or any other faith-based work for that matter—knowing the purpose of the work is crucial to doing it well. Why are we helping these people in the first place? What is our end goal? What are the required benchmarks? Scripture offers many possible starting points for such questions. There's the good news of God's reign (Matthew 10:7), help for the marginalized as succor for the Messiah himself (Matthew 25:40), and being witnesses of Jesus moving about the earth (Acts 1:8)—to name a few. From there, plan a road map based on your community and core strengths.

Our mission statement at the Border Church is "to follow Jesus and seek the reign of God by breaking bread along and across the San Diego-Tijuana border." From there, we contextualize biblical motifs related to the *basileia* and use this mission as a road guide along our way to the ministry's vision, which is "That God's love would reign over the US-Mexico borderlands so that all people, sitting together at a common table, would experience heaven on earth." So, not only is the mission founded upon God's *basileia*, but the vision aims to broaden the experience of the *basileia* for many in this place.

Knowing the Sights

To do their job well, the tour guide must spend an appropriate amount of time at each site. Digging deeper at specific points and knowing which sights to see or skip requires a mastery of the local terrain. The what and the how of conveying essential points of interest make the tour worth attending. The traveler can enjoy it and learn along the way.

Every effective priest, activist, and community organizer knows that nothing is possible in a community without first knowing that community and the principles its members are trying to employ within it. The people we seek to serve require more than just nice words; they need to know that we have something to offer them, whether it be assistance, knowledge, or a way to take action. Their time with us may not always be enjoyable, but there have to be moments for joy, hope, and love while we walk together.

Knowing the Tourists

One of my favorite parts of going on a tour is talking to the guide between sights to find out more about something we just saw or about their personal backstory. Such a human connection makes me enjoy the experience even more. The same is true for the few times I've given a border tour. Knowing my audience helps me better connect with them. Guillermo is a rock star at this. He makes those on the bus feel valued, whether they've just taken a first-class southward flight from their prestigious university town or fled death threats and walked thousands of kilometers northward.

They all have a deep need to feel that we simply know and appreciate them. It may not be a personal relationship, but it does have to be a human-to-human connection over time. It's about more than just getting the task done for some person or group. We have to accompany them along their journeys.

I believe you have what it takes to accompany those in need along your own tour of the *basileia*, and I'd love to hear your stories of doing so. You can email me at SethDavidClark@gmail.com, and I'll do my best to respond. In so doing, we can accompany one another and share—at least digital—bread for the journey.

NOTES

1. See "Accompany (v.)," *Online Etymology Dictionary*, https://www.etymonline.com/word/accompany. See also "Company (n.)," *Online Etymology Dictionary*, https://www.etymonline.com/word/company.
2. *Richard Rohr: Essential Teachings on Love*, ed. Joelle Chase and Judy Traeger (Maryknoll, NY: Orbis Books, 2018), 65, 102–103.

CHAPTER 6

A FRIEND OF A FRIEND OF GOD

I have known Daniel "Dan" Watman for a few years. He's a regular attendee of the Border Church in addition to being the best Spanish teacher I've ever had. As a person who has chosen a life on the southern side of the fence, Dan is among a growing number of non-Hispanic US citizens who call Tijuana home. Like him, many do so for economic reasons. Unlike most expats in the area, however, Dan lives there with a deeper purpose than personal finance. His life's goal is to work for transnational justice through cross-border encounters and friendships, especially at Friendship Park. He lives within a stone's throw of the border fence, a few minutes' walk from El Faro.

Having resided more than twenty years on one side or the other of the border, Dan knows these borderlands exceptionally well. He sees the border itself as one particularly exceptional feature, and the Friendship Park stretch of that border is where he has concentrated his efforts to create cross-border friendships for quite some time. Dan tells me, "When I discovered Friendship Park, it was just a chain-link fence and a border. Now, there's an eighteen-foot fence." In fact, as I write this, it was only days ago that President Biden paused the construction of a thirty-foot secondary fence that had been encroaching upon that same space. Dan laments certain unjust changes at the border, especially the posture of federal authorities: "You used to be able to just show up and do an event. Now you can't do that. It's a totally different place than how it was." Underneath this observation is a desire for greater justice on *la frontera*.

While living in San Diego, Dan's growing involvement with Friendship Park made him notice the ways in which regulations were getting more and more restrictive. The change made it apparent that if he wanted to stay involved with the Binational Friendship Garden, which he started in 2007, Dan would have to do more on the Mexican side. He knew he had to make Tijuana his home, yet he did not realize how much meaning he had attached to his personal identity of being from the United States. So, he went through an identity crisis as he learned what it meant to be a US citizen in Tijuana. Dan tells me that through this period, he "got a little taste of what it's like to go to a foreign country. 'Am I from here? Am I from there?,'" Unlike the migrants arriving out of desperation, though, he knows he had a choice.

A sense of identity and belonging is crucial for doing justice work well. Knowing who you are helps you know the boundaries between yourself and others. Injustice too commonly occurs when we forget who we are and when we forget that other individuals are also primarily defined by their relationship to God.

To Dan, San Diego is a spread-out, isolated, and individualistic place. Dan's communalistic approach to friendship and justice is more in line with a *basileia* ethic than that of the individualistic spirit so present in US culture. He contrasts US individualism in San Diego with Tijuana.

As Dan sees it, the southern sister city is much more social and connected. He feels like there is a grassroots vibe in Tijuana that is less prevalent in San Diego, with burgeoning arts, environmental justice, and human rights scenes. Dan admits it might just be the circles he runs in, but it appears to be true nonetheless. Though he sees the advantages of the isolation and quiet that San Diego offers, especially as he grows older, Dan still prefers the hustle, bustle, and connectivity of Tijuana over the suburban feel of its northern neighbor.

What Dan likes most about the borderlands is the people. He sees young people who are "super inspired and motivated. They're dreamers for a bigger and better world." These activated aspirations can be found in the groups and organizations Dan encounters all over. Additionally, he sees and appreciates the region's global nature because of the "people arriving all the time from all over the world." Dan recognizes the hardship stemming from the root of their needing to come as he points out the "horrible circumstances that made them come here." Yet, he sees the goodness in interacting with people who have come directly from another culture. Dan says, "It's like seeing the world through their culture and language's framework. It makes me feel good to be able to use my privilege to be able to help other people who are in need."

In these interlingual, intercultural, and intersectional spaces, Dan recognizes that his twofold desire to learn languages and to help others fits right in. Dan intentionally works with migrant-serving groups such as the Border Church and the Binational Friendship Garden—both of which can be found along either side of the wall at Friendship Park. On the southern side of the garden, Dan often strikes up relationships with those living temporarily in the nearby canyons. He shares whatever resources he can with the people he meets. If that isn't verging on *basileia* life, I'm not sure what is.

Dan's neighbors are his favorite aspect of the local borderlands, but it is the border itself that he likes least. Moreover, he finds the Border Patrol and US border policy to be suffocating; there is no room for the friendship across the border that he believes wholeheartedly is the best avenue to safety. For Dan, enforcement does not equate to security. Instead, it is familiarity and friendship that people and nations require for real security. I think he's right; the best justice is one complete with a posture of openness toward the other.

As far as Dan's own spiritual background, Dan tells me that he grew up not following any religion or spiritual path. His dad is Jewish. His mom grew up Catholic. Maybe for that reason they decided not to raise their children in either religion. However, they offered some exposure to both—one synagogue service and one mass as well as weddings and other life events grounded in religion. All in all, Dan acknowledges, "It's never been a part of my practice. . . . It still isn't really."

Looking back, what drew this non-religious person to the Border Church was his alignment with some of its principles—and of religion in general—without any decision or concerted effort to become religious personally. I see this overlap of principles in Dan's telling of the Border Church's origin story. As a replacement wall was being erected and threatening to cut off cross-border interaction, Dan contacted John Fanestil because he knew of his religious work and advocacy and wanted to team up to do something to maintain cross-border access. The wall was coming too fast, though, to keep things as they had been. So, Dan tells me they decided to put all their eggs in one basket: Friendship Park. Along the way, John was serving communion through the fence until he got arrested for doing that, and

the Friends of Friendship Park, which both Dan and John
have been a part of, got behind the Border Church's effort.

Even without aligning himself with John's religion, Dan
tells me he started seeing that their principles were wholly
aligned. They had different motivations—"his were that
God wanted to do it, mine were that I wanted to"—but
either way, Dan wanted to stop the wall just like John did.
Dan tells me that this Border Church involvement was the
start of his closest-ever affiliation with religion.

Through the years, Dan recounts how he and John have
been trying to get more access to the park in a two-pronged
approach that includes the Border Church and the binational garden. Dan believes that the Border Church has done
more, but the garden is there, too, and that's his baby. He
says, "We're both trying to get more access. It kept me close
to religion, I guess, because I love what John would say,
[preaching] passages in the Bible that fit my perspective of
what needs to happen in the world." Dan did not necessarily believe he was becoming religious, but he certainly saw
himself identifying with religious folks and their messages of
unity and friendship.

For Dan, a relationship with God is not as public as it is
personal. He says he is "not into publicly worshiping." He
considers himself an agnostic and tells me that if there is a
God, the point is "more about doing good than worshiping
God." He confesses that he goes back and forth sometimes,
though, and that understanding God as an actual external
entity can be helpful.

I've asked Dan to describe Christianity in the past. It
admittedly stumped him at first: "Well, Christianity—oh,
my God—I don't understand it. It's way too complicated,
to be honest." Dan eventually told me that all he can say
is that following what feels right and what feels like doing
good ends up connecting him with portions of the Christian
faith. He has reservations, though, because of the horrible

things done in the name of Christianity and how spiritual beliefs seem more individual than institutional.

Because the Border Church is his only longstanding Christian experience, Dan is hesitant to describe church because he does not have enough exposure to feel confident in providing an accurate description. Regardless, he has been in Mexico for some time and uses that experience to talk about local Catholic practices. Dan recounts how his *compadre*,[1] someone he tells me is the closest person to blood family he has in Mexico, leaned over to him in the middle of a baptism that Dan was an integral part of and told him, "This is a bunch of crap." To Dan, this seems typical. Some people view Christianity as a tradition more than a religion; they will answer that they believe in Jesus Christ when asked and assume Sunday should be the day off, but their spirituality does not go much deeper.

For Dan, the Border Church seems different. He sums it up with a sense of fondness and wonder: "Wow, it's great . . . It's become such a way for people to connect." He contrasts the cross-border connection that the church fosters with other initiatives he has been a part of at Friendship Park. Dan remembers the frustrations of trying to plan things like yoga that were meant to unite people through the fence but ended up uniting the organizers more than the participants. Yet the Border Church being on-site and involved has caused cross-fence exchanges to flourish more, according to Dan, partly because of Guillermo's suggestion to make use of sound equipment that can bring people together more effectively in a space designed to separate.

More broadly, Dan tells me that the Border Church's goals and his are the same as far as making friends and having a human connection across the border. He says, "That's what Border Church is all about. Everyone is God's child. God doesn't see the separation. God sees the connection." Dan wants those things, too: family, unity, and connection.

"Having so many people there with that perspective—and this sounds funny—is kind of a Godsend," says Dan, who firmly believes this weekly practice is the thing that gives the most hope that the wall can come down.

Dan thinks the Border Church's setting and aim make it completely different from other churches. He has never heard of a church without a roof, and beyond that, he says, "I know for sure that there's no other church whose regular meeting place is across an international border." There may be other churches straddling borders, but there is none to my knowledge that meets on both sides of such a highly weaponized and walled-off international boundary.

One time, Dan and I dove deep into the denominational realities that he has no regard for, such as how our friend Guillermo, who at that point sat within earshot, cannot preside at communion without a duly ordained minister present. Dan decided that he'd let the religious people figure that stuff out. This friend of mine prefers to focus on the point of what happens at the Border Church, saying: "All I know is that Guillermo is, like, one of the most dedicated people I've seen in my life. He's very dedicated to his religion. He's very dedicated to helping migrants. And that's all I care about." Moments later, he declared, "I think the Border Church is badass," and "I like the content of it . . . to me, that's what's great about it. If that content can grow, I feel like institutional support can fall where it may." Can my friend get an amen?

For Dan, the practice of communion is about friendship. His favorite part of the entire service is when someone says: "Turn to someone on the other side and make a friend, basically." This is what the pinky-kiss sign of peace before communion at the wall means for Dan. He does not usually take communion, because according to him, it is not a personal tradition. He supports the Border Church's efforts so much that when he has participated in communion, it was to show his solidarity. What initially attracted Dan, who had never thought he would be tempted to participate in church ceremonies, was John's reading of scriptures and preaching. Dan explains what he means: "It didn't seem like he was preaching the Bible. It seemed like he was preaching a point of view that was necessary and missing in the border narrative and supporting himself with passages from the Bible."

Even a statement like that shows that Dan has a very different understanding of the Bible than many readers have. So, what is a church to do with a friend of a friend of God? Beyond the bits about justice and *basileia* mentioned above, two biblical-theological concepts come to my mind: friendship and the nations and the mission. My friend Dan embodies both of those concepts.

Friend

Friend, or *amiga/o,* is a broadly defined term. So, how am I using it? I studied early Christianity in graduate school, so I do know a fair bit of Greek. Of the handful of Greek terms that translate to "friend" in English or *amiga/o* in Spanish, the most common term is φίλος (*philos*). It's in the Christian scriptures nearly thirty times, and its verbal form φιλέω (*phileō*) appears more than twenty times.

The word *philos* was an essential word for early Christians. Literally, philos translates to "a loved one." It's not merely a friend. To love someone with the *philos* kind of friendship is to love someone as a sibling. Every word has a wide breadth of meaning, called the semantic range, so it was not every single time someone was called a companion in the *philos* way that they were being regarded as family. Still, the familial root was present from the word's meaning throughout the scriptural texts of our early Christian predecessors.

When Pastor John presides at communion along the fence, he routinely draws our hands and eyes to the sky to remind us between a prayer of confession and reminder of pardon that we all live under one open sky as one human family made by God. That's an apt starting place for those who wouldn't self-describe as Christian. They are part of the human family, and they are children of the Creator. As humans, we share in the one family of our species as the only kind of creature made in God's image. Hence, we have in our nature the grounds for *philos* friendship.

What does it mean, then, when some of our friends wouldn't necessarily identify with the One who now calls his followers friends (John 15:15)? Can the friends of Christ's followers be friends of God too?

Love is a choice. God chooses to love all people. That's the promise we have in Jesus. Some Christian universalists, like the Eastern Orthodox scholar David Bentley Hart, argue that all humans are created by God to love God, which ensures they will love God eventually. The guarantee of this love also ensures every human's salvation.[2] Other Christian thinkers, often in the Calvinist tradition, argue that some people are left purposefully unchosen by God and thereby are unable to love God. Many Christians in the middle of the two perspectives think love is a choice, and such love can be withheld from God.

Whatever your opinion is about humans' ability to choose to love God, you may well never see friends and family make a choice to love God the same way you do. Yet, if you are God's *amiga* or *amigo*, each remains a friend of a friend of God. To be a friend with someone does require each party to agree to that friendship. Yet, I'd argue that being in God's extended friend network is a pretty decent place to be. It brings the friend of a friend closer to the *basileia* that God is ushering in right here and right now.

Mi amigo Dan is all about promoting friendship along and across the San Diego-Tijuana border. Although he may not consider fellowship with the Divine important, my God has friendly vibes—*philos* even—toward Dan. As the friend in the middle, I don't feel the need to foster their relationship, but I also don't need to be ashamed of my friend or friendship. I can talk about the good news of God's *basileia* when Dan is at the Border Church, and I can tell God in my prayers how grateful I am for Dan and all his good borderlands work.

Nations

Throughout the scriptures, we read about the "nations." Sometimes also translated as "Gentiles," original ancient terms (the plural of גּוֹיִם/*goyim*, עַמִּים/*ammim*, and לְאֻמִּים/ *lĕʾūmmîm* in Hebrew and ἔθνη/*ethnē* in Greek) basically refer to non-Jews. In the Christian tradition, the term has also come to refer to those who are not followers of the God of Abraham, Isaac, and Jacob. The same God and Divine Parent is thought of through it all, but the people of God move from an ethnic Israelite group alone to one that includes them plus all other tribes and peoples.

If we can put on the interpretive lenses of nations as all those who are blessed by the people of God (Genesis 22:18), we can find some fascinating readings for the friends of the friends of God. Though some Hebrew scriptural authors and redactors included more than a bit of ambivalence toward the nations, we find an incredibly hopeful strand of prophetic vision from the Hebrew scriptures to those of the Hebrew Christians.

The Lexham Bible Dictionary has helpfully compiled some biblical texts with examples of Israel's hope in God for all peoples. The Mosaic Law commanded compassion toward foreigners (Leviticus 19:33-34; Deuteronomy 10:18-19). There are prophecies that the nations shall eventually come to partake in the worship of YHWH, the God of Israel (Psalm 22:27-28; compare 47:1-4 and 96:7-9). We find that Isaiah wrote how "all nations and all tongues" will one day join with YHWH, minister to this true God, love and serve God, observe the Sabbath, abide by the covenant, come to pray in the temple, and even make offerings and sacrifices to the Lord (Isaiah 56:6-7; 66:18-21).[3]

From this point on, the biblical outlook seems to build to an increasingly hopeful tone regarding Gentile nations. Jumping ahead to the last book of the canon—and likely the last New Testament book written—Revelation, we see a future in which the author John looks and finds that individuals from every tribe, language, people, and nation come together. They do so to worship the crucified and resurrected Lamb of God in heaven (Revelation 5:6-10). John expects the holy reign of God to be wholly consummated. When that occurs, all the nations of the earth will walk in the presence and light of Divinity. The earth's rulers will also bring into the heavenly city "the glory and honor of the nations" (Revelation 21:24-26). John envisions the tree of life fully restored. Its leaves will, like in the times of Adam and Eve, be for healing, but this time they are "for the healing of the nations" (Revelation 22:2). This is the hope of the *basileia* fully consummated.

Through the hermeneutical lenses of hope and love, it becomes apparent that the Bible is arguing that all the nations will be united in hope fulfilled and love made tangible. The friends of the people of God can, thereby, claim such hope for themselves. Those who are seekers or skeptics but still associating with the people of God doing God's work may not fully align with our thoughts and beliefs, but when they align with our hopes and goals for justice, we can gladly accept them as friends of another "nation." Like in the offspring of Abraham and within the unifying writings of the prophets, we can seek to be a blessing to them. In doing so, as Jesus has done and will do again, we tear down the barriers too quickly constructed by societies and cultures.

Mission

Speaking of what Jesus did and will do again, he surprised a lot of the religious people in his day because he partnered with unlikely characters. He hung out with sinners, prostitutes, extorting tax collectors, lowly fishers, one-time demoniacs, and even Gentiles. These kinds of people were all on the lower levels of the societal and religious ladder. All of these lowly outsiders helped Jesus on his mission. So too can the friend of the friend of God.

Jesus once said that whoever was not against us was for us (Mark 9:40). Many of our friends with whom we are on a justice mission certainly do not seem to be against Jesus or his followers, at least as it pertains to defending the rights of the downtrodden.

Furthermore, Jesus commanded his followers to be shrewd by using their wealth to make friends (Luke 16:9). That likely refers to almsgiving—a practice of direct giving to the neediest that the church has lost touch with in its programmatic giving campaigns and funds. Regardless, making friends with others who are also using their resources for the good of those in a lowly estate is no haphazard extension of the passage. When we are on a mission with friends for justice, our rationales may differ, but the justice that we can reach before the Restorer of Justice returns is still real and realizable. As such, even if not fully realized, true justice is worthy of partnership with the friends of the friends of God.

NOTES

1. A *compadre* is the father of one's godchild.
2. David Bentley Hart, *That All Shall Be Saved: Heaven, Hell, and Universal Salvation* (New Haven, CT: Yale University Press, 2019).
3. Dennis L. Durst, "Nations, the," ed. John D. Barry et al., *The Lexham Bible Dictionary* (Bellingham, WA: Lexham Press, 2016).

CHAPTER 7

BEYOND AWOKENING

A Free Verse Autobiography

To be woke is to be awakened to injustice,
Tho' widening both eyes is not enough.
I can think, say, and click correctly,
Yet wokeness won't end walls.
Kinship gazes awaken vision;
Pinky kisses stir my soul.
I cannot not act now.
Transformed.
I'm no savior here.
In divided humans, I see the One.
Incorporating Divinity, we become one.
I share bread and cup (and bread again when I can).
Like John, I preach: "Repent for the *basileia* of God
    is at hand!"
Like Jesus, I pray: "Thy will be done at the border
    as it is in heaven."
I am become Christ at the fence. They are become
    Christ to me at the wall.

CHAPTER 8

FIERCELY MAKING PEACE

Robert is an addict. He makes his way in the world, knowing that at any moment, he could slip and fall back into the lifestyle that got him deported. He's seen it happen with others, even past mentors. Like many recovering addicts, Robert has given up on street drugs but has found a new craving: he works for the good of those in very bad situations. His mind and body once waged war against him with cravings, but now Robert wages war on injustice to make peace at the border. Below is his story.

Robert Vivar was born on June 17, 1956, in Tijuana, Baja California, Mexico, where he now resides. Though he was born there, he has not always been a Tijuanan. Like many other US immigrants, Robert legally came to California at six years of age. His family settled in the southern California city of Corona, not too far away from Los Angeles. His pattern of being on the move did not end in Corona; Robert's life brought him to Los Angeles as well as Tucson, Las Vegas, and Chicago.

What makes Robert's story a true *historia fronteriza* (border story) is that he is now back. Many migrants enter and leave Tijuana as economic and familial fortunes ebb and flow, but Robert's homecoming to Tijuana was not of his own volition. Robert got deported. Twice. Getting deported twice seldom is a recipe for successful legal re-entry into the United States. So, Tijuana is home for as long as Robert's deportation order remains in effect. Though lawyers have brought the underlying conviction that led to the first deportation before the California State Supreme Court, Robert may never again be allowed to step foot in the country he calls home.

Robert has always been a go-getter. After a childhood and youth spent in the California public school system, Robert used his education and drive to work his way up the corporate ladder. While working at AeroMexico, he started inching closer to finding his own identity as both Mexican and American. It was only after returning to Tijuana that he found it. He puts it this way:

> Growing up in the US, you grow up not knowing who you are or liking who you are, but you play behind a façade. Because of the color of my skin, I could look and act Anglo. I didn't want to receive the slurs that I saw my other co-nationals receive. A lot of that was from Hispanic people born in the US.
>
> I guess that sometimes I was ashamed of my culture and who I really was. You know, my mom would get up early in the morning and work her tail off to get breakfast ready for us, lunch ready for us. . . . So that I wouldn't be made fun of, I threw my lunch away. I was growing up not liking myself fully.
>
> As I got out of high school and started working at Aero-Mexico airline, I started feeling at home with my home people. Once I moved here and started getting involved in activism, I started to get to know the true person, the true Robert—what I like and what I wanted to do. You know, at that time, I wanted to appear white and not brown, and now I am who I am. I feel like I belong here because that's where I was born. But at the same time, I feel like I belong in the US too because I was raised there. I belong to both countries, and both countries belong to me.

Finding peace with who he really is has taken much of his life, but, in doing so, he has been able to root himself in both nations and bear much fruit where they meet. Right after this shared self-reflection, Robert sheds light on a powerful self-realization: "The Robert who exists now is a person who is seeking justice and seeking value in life and in families."

That is not the Robert of AeroMexico. The former Robert was addicted to success. Even without a college degree, his wit and determination propelled the businessman up the corporate ladder. He confesses he was "doing drugs and running around with women." Eventually, a voice inside him said: "Look what you're doing to your loved ones." So, he decided never to hurt them in this way again. Unfortunately, because of an unforgiving criminal justice and immigration system, his newfound commitment came too late.

It came after a drug charge and a plea deal. Robert never denies having used hard drugs; his addiction even caused him to be homeless for a time. But Robert was misinformed about what the plea deal would mean for his immigration status. He regrets never having applied for US citizenship because if he had, he believes his immigration status wouldn't have been an issue. For non-citizen immigrants and green card holders, drug crimes often carry automatic deportation orders. Hard-earned lives in the United States become wedged between the rock of substance abuse and the hard place of the War on Drugs. This undeniably disastrous predicament impacts far too many migrants and other marginalized groups in our society.

Robert Vivar wanted to make things right when he was deported. He didn't want to become another statistic. He wanted most of all to do right by his family, and he couldn't do that in Mexico. So, he successfully crossed from one California to another without documentation. Upon arriving back home, he started to make a new life for himself.

Before this all took place, Robert had a bit of a spiritual conversion. Though he had grown up in a family of faith, he says his addiction took him so far away from that faith-formed moral core that he began dehumanizing himself. If a life of virtue makes one more like Christ, a life of indulgence and addiction leads one away from the God who always seeks to save those who are lost.

Robert had arrived in ICE detention devoid of inner peace. There, a mini-miracle happened. He recounts this whole story as follows:

> I grew up, of course, believing in God. Thinking that I believed in God. Believing in Christ. Thinking that I believed in Christ. I knew he existed, and I prayed to him once in a while, but that was about it.
>
> When the relationship began was when I was arrested for one of the first times. And I was put in a two-man cell. When I saw how small it was, I got claustrophobic. I wanted to pound on the door and tell them I was going to die. The top bunk had me inches from the ceiling. Beyond that, I was thinking about my wife and my kids. I started almost to hyperventilate. I just lay there. Time stopped. I was thinking: "I gotta do something. What can I do?" I figured there might be a book under the mat. I had seen the Bible, but I was scared to read the Bible because people said it was scary. So, I was like: "Ahh, boy. Okay." But this anxiety was so strong that I couldn't breathe. So, I tried it. The more I read, the more I was relaxed. "This is good. I like this!" A day or two later, I was like, "I'm getting out of this jail or I'm getting out of this cell." So, I went to the [church] service, and it was great. And the more I read, the better I felt.

In the New Testament letter to the church at Colossae, the author urges the Colossians in 3:15 to let the peace of Christ reign over their lives. I am convinced this is the same peace that Robert had been missing and then found—in an ICE detention center. In the very next Christ-centered command, found in the following verse, the author urges the

Colossians to let Christ's word dwell richly in them. These commands—letting Christ's peace reign and Christ's words remain—are not identical, but they are related. Even while Robert was behind bars, he found them cooperating for his benefit.

Yes, Robert found peace, but it wasn't because everything unfolded exactly as he planned. Nor did his peace result in everything working out as he wanted. Had the War on Drugs or the drugs' war on Robert's mind ended? No. Was Robert completely mended by the mini-miracle of finding a Bible and a measure of peace therein? Probably not. Did his immigration status troubles go away? Absolutely not. And yet, he found peace—Christ's peace.

Robert thought at that moment in 2003 that he was going to stay close to God. It didn't quite work out that way. Life moved on and he got distracted, but God was always there. Robert never returned to a life of drugs, but he had not fully surrendered his life to God as he felt he should. Instead, he was always trying to make a deal with God.

In Robert's own words, here's what happened next:

> I got back across [into the US] and was living without documentation. I wasn't perfect, but I cleaned up my act. I thought I had a deal with God that if I remained that way (working for my family), I'd not get arrested. But a few months before I got deported again, my now ex-wife and I had talked about helping homeless people. It was God, but I didn't listen.
>
> Eventually, ICE picked me up. At that moment, I told myself: "No matter how long I'm in jail, I'm fighting this. They're not going to deport me."
>
> I got help from a lawyer to represent myself, and I started to work on my case.
>
> There were several church services in the detention center. We got the same Bible study that had impacted me so profoundly my first time in detention back up and running even though there had been problems between Catholics and other Christians [which tore it apart].

I was asking God what he wanted me to do, but again I was negotiating with him. I'd say: "Tell me what you want me to do, but help me with my case so that I can go back to my family."

Eventually, I came back to my senses. If I got deported, there was something that God wanted me to do. I had faith that I would get back home, but I knew I would have to accept and embrace it if I got deported. That happened on Good Friday, 2013. I had a better plan this time.

I was working in Tijuana. I was trying to keep things together with my wife back on the other side. I even started saving money for the first time. I was trying to take my wife to Cabo so she wouldn't leave me. I was trying to find a church, but it didn't work.

On December 25th of the same year that I got deported the second time, my wife told me that she was leaving me for another man.

Eventually, I came to my senses after fighting with God. "Who the hell am I to question? Why should I even ask why?" So, I said: "Yeah, I'm ready."

One day, while walking out of a church, a church I was not comfortable in, I saw a sign for deported veterans. My son is active-duty. Other family members are veterans. I started getting hooked up with Border Angels, and their people started showing me the activism ropes and put me in touch with Guillermo from the Border Church.

Mind you, by this time I had terrible depression. Couldn't work. Couldn't eat. Couldn't sleep. When I started getting involved, I started feeling better. The more I got involved, the more I felt better. I was doing what I knew God wanted me to do.

When I first got involved in activism, a fellow activist took me to Border Church, and I was like: "This is it!"

When I listen to Robert or reflect on his words, I see God at work. I see a flawed family man created in God's image, trying to do right by his kin even if that means breaking the law. I see someone growing in holiness. I see a national system that has historically failed to grant justice for the oppressed. In its failure to do what God requires, it unwittingly points to the very God who is just.

Because this chapter is about peace, let's hone in on the waxing and waning of peace in Robert's life and compare his situation to a biblical character whose own fortunes also shifted radically during his lifetime. David might seem like an odd pick. Why not someone like Job, who lost it all? Or maybe one of the prophets who got forced out of their home country? Here's why. The supposed "man after God's own heart" had a life full of many good and bad fortunes as well as many consequences of political and familial intrigue—only some of which he had control over. All the while, he is said to have offered dozens of the Judeo-Christian tradition's oldest hymns and worship songs in the book of Psalms. Some are filled with peace. Others are full of hate and internal angst. David was a leader of mercenary armies and a man of war. So, it is difficult to argue that this man of God was filled with the peace of Christ spoken about in later testaments of divine grace.

The contrasts between King David and Robert Vivar are obvious. The former is an ancient Hebrew warlord from roughly three thousand years ago; the latter is a first-generation Mexican-American living in the present day. King David was a shepherd-turned-king; Robert was an airline employee-turned-deportee. The ancient songwriter's most apparent sins were adultery and angering the Lord for taking the Israelite census; Robert's were womanizing and drug abuse.

Here are some similarities, though. David lived in exile in forests, in deserts, and with the hated Philistines because he feared for his life under a murderous ruler, King Saul. While Robert didn't flee the United States or its ruling regime, he was exiled to Mexico after his conviction. Both David and Robert are people who could not feel at home in their own homes. They lived in liminal spaces. Even after

David had been king for some time, he was uprooted again when his son Absalom mounted a temporarily successful *coup d'état*. After being deported once, Robert came back to his family for a season before being picked up by federal agents again—this time under false pretenses.

Speaking of family drama, David and his several wives had numerous conflicts of their own. In ancient Semitic culture, it was virtually unheard of for a woman to divorce a man. It simply did not happen, but I can only imagine some of David's actions causing a modern spouse to walk away from that marriage. Robert did not live under the archaic customs and laws codified in the late Bronze Age to force his estranged wife to stay. She had her own choice when conflict arose. Even when he sought to make amends, it was not enough. It was too late to save his relationship. Her decision was set.

When I read the accounts of David in 1 and 2 Samuel and 1 Chronicles, I cannot help but wonder what was going on inside his head. When I read the Psalms that ancient Jews determined were his, I still don't see much peace. I see a desire for it. I feel the longing David has to be at home in the world of praise and at peace in the house of the Lord. Yet, David's bloody hands were too stained even to build the Lord a proper temple.

When I listen to Robert's story and reflect on the time we've spent together, I am graced with the thought that I have experienced the *basileia* with and through his friendship. Like David, Robert wants peace. I believe monarchial intrigue never let David settle down into that life of worship he wanted, but Robert doesn't have a kingdom on his back. A similarity here, though, is that Robert's "temple" is incomplete. It only has one wall, and he cannot cross to the other side of it. That longing keeps peace at arm's length.

King David's life ended after a story full of ups and downs. Robert has experienced rock bottom but has since bounced back in ways his former self could only dream of. It is an upside-down story—the kind often found in the *basileia*.

Professionally, Robert has never regained the powerful corporate position that he had before the consequences of a drug addiction took it all away. Yet, I can tell that he is more fulfilled now than ever before. He's earning a paycheck by working for both Via International and the Border Church. I'm sure the Tijuana salary is not what the executive-level US compensation package was. Still, a world of change in his heart has made Robert appreciate that there's more to life than a lucrative career. Why else would he be doing this work of sending deported veterans back to the United States?

After his wife left him, Robert didn't know if he could ever love again. The ideologies that he had coming out of a conservative church and culture made him think moving on would be sinful. Eventually, though, Robert found love with Blanca. Robert has made a new home in Mexico with Blanca, her biological daughter, and their adopted daughter from Honduras. Because Robert's own daughter back in the United States is addicted to drugs, his Honduran daughter holds a special place in his life. He keeps in touch with some of his biological family members, but because he was deported, he cannot travel to see them. Since some family members live far away or have busy lives, they don't often make their way down to Tijuana to see Robert. Though his lack of familial engagement saddens him, Robert's "adopted family," as he calls those in his life now, are people he can care for and who care for him.

When peering through the border fence, I've seen Blanca at the Border Church nearly as much as Robert. Blanca has a maternal, approachable demeanor that draws people in with kindness and genuine care. Her participation in the *basileia* on the Mexican side is vital for deported moms, migrants, and many others. It's no wonder she and Robert hit it off. Together they care for the common good through tangible acts of accompaniment.

What drew me to explore Robert's by way of the concept of peace was not just his work for a positive home life or a satisfying work life but his activism on behalf of deported US warriors and their peace. Robert is the co-director of the Unified US Deported Veterans Resource Center and vice president of the Tijuana chapter of Veterans for Peace. A father of an active-duty airman himself, Robert knows all too well that military life is hard enough as it is. Deportation after their service robs US veterans of the peace they earned in this nation by fighting for it.

In the past, if you served honorably in the United States Armed Forces, you would be able to settle down in the country you served with the full confidence that the nation would have your back. This is no longer the case. Some of the same women and men who fought for our country—many having suffered the physical and mental wounds of combat in Vietnam, Iraq, and Afghanistan—have found that the country they were willing to die for is unwilling to put up with them. Within the past two decades, federal laws changed so that a non-citizen veteran who was found guilty of certain types of crimes would be eligible for deportation. Hundreds have been deported. Many still live as close to the US as possible with the hope of returning. Others have moved on beyond the border region. Few have returned to the US alive, though their veteran benefits do give them one hope of return: their corpses may be buried in a plot of US soil after they die. Even within this grim reality, there is still hope; as I write this, the current presidential administration has started making a path for many deported veterans to return to the country they served. I'm hopeful that you, reader, will know the good news (or history) as your eyes grace these words. For now, though, there is no simple path out of this injustice.

Veterans often got into deportable legal trouble as a direct or indirect result of the mental anguish caused by terror on the battlefield. That doesn't matter according to the laws of the land, however, as deported vets now cannot even access the physical or mental healthcare they've earned as veterans of the United States military. Generally speaking, the fact that the only veteran benefit that deported US veterans have left is the opportunity to be buried in the land they swore an oath to protect is a travesty—one that Robert fights every way he can.

The veterans served their time in the armed forces. They served their time behind bars for any crimes committed after getting out. They served. The nation they and I both call home returns their service with the incredible disservice of deportation. To fight this injustice, Robert leads others to call on elected officials to change unjust laws. Some candidates and legislators have even come down to Mexico to speak with and advocate for those involved in the work. Sadly, too much of it is lip service. Few federal bills have emerged to change the laws so that deported veterans can come home. None that I know of have even been voted on in both chambers of Congress, much less touched the desk of the armed services' Commander in Chief.

Yet, Robert and his comrades-in-peace fight on. Not only do they fight to change an unjust system, but they also work for individuals and families impacted by it. For example, some deported veterans arrive in Mexico no longer speaking the language of their parents. Then, too many arrive without proper Mexican documents to live and work in their country of birth since they've been gone so long—without the ability to speak with government officials or read the necessary paperwork. According to Robert, because the bureaucratic systems in Mexico can be worse than those of the US, getting residency in a Mexican city like Tijuana is a difficult task whether or not you know the native tongue. So he helps with translation or simply with filling out paperwork whenever needed. Robert can't singlehandedly fix the system, but he can help people navigate it along the way.

Equipped with health kits and helpful tips, the Unified US Deported Veterans Resource Center, which Robert simply refers to as "the office," serves as a space to help veterans and others who are newly deported or experiencing other hardships. I've witnessed people in crisis coming into the center, hoping that someone will be able to help them. With a health·kit and maybe some snacks in hand, Robert and his team quickly provide friendship and comfort during the lowest points of their patrons' lives. This caring triage occurs only meters away from the San Ysidro border crossing and its deportation drop-off point. Robert and his comrades seek to make things right and to continuously engage with a public that too easily moves on from this unrighteous reality. In doing so, they cultivate grounds for peace—little by little.

In the fight against a very peculiar and particular form of injustice, Robert uses his deftness as an organizer and leader to rally the troops of volunteer activists with whom he stands. Just as Robert has experienced, the veterans he serves now deal with two national systems and all of the structural inequities within them. If you're wondering what you can do about these inequities, keep in mind that with the power of your votes, calls, and emails to representatives, you can help Robert and other deportees find a little more justice, a slightly greater chance for thriving, and a better opportunity for peace. Are you brave enough to stand on the side of justice in a battle for peace?

I admit that I haven't been as active as I sometimes feel I should, given my moral code and participation in border work. Robert often asks for simple acts that I can do as a US citizen. I've written emails, I've made calls, and I've even sat down with congressional staffers. But I don't consider myself an activist. It took me a while to muster up the courage even to write to my representatives. Sometimes I still put this holy work off because it feels uncomfortable. But it still needs to be done. I still need to remember that my sisters and brothers in Tijuana need people like me to use my voice for their sake. I need to follow Robert into this battle and pray that peace meets us and those we fight for on the other side.

Robert's story is typified by the inner peace of a saint or the victory of a war hero. Still, he has been working for peace in his life and the lives of others on the margins of two societies. The odd truth I see in him, though, is that peace doesn't always come through victory.

In the Sermon on the Mount, which is all about God's *basileia*, Jesus specifically mentioned the blessedness or happiness of the peacemakers as children of God (Matthew 5:9). So, what does it mean to make peace? The last chapter of Philippians shows that it's God's will to have God's peace (Philippians 4:7,9), and Jesus himself told his followers that those who make peace are blessed and happy (Matthew 5:9). The concept is all over the scriptures and embedded deep within certain theological traditions from Christ's time to ours, yet we don't always seem to get it. Instead, we are preoccupied with the worries of our everyday life and, worse still, things outside of our control.

The peace of God that the church at Philippi promised for us is no small thing. The fourth- and fifth-century Doctor of the Church, and one of my favorite ancient Bible expositors, St. John Chrysostom, describes the vastness and depth of this promise as follows:

> *The peace of God which He hath wrought toward men, surpasseth all understanding. For who could have expected, who could have hoped, that such good things would have come?*

They exceed all man's understanding, not his speech alone. For His enemies, for those who hated Him, for those who determined to turn themselves away, for these, he refused not to deliver up His Only Begotten Son, that He might make peace with us. This peace then, i.e., the reconciliation, the love of God, shall guard your hearts and your thoughts.[1]

Chrysostom continues expounding on what we could easily argue is the *basileia* by saying that Christ has delivered us by means beyond our comprehension and also guards our hearts. Chrysostom also reminds the hearer how in John 14:27, Jesus promised he was leaving his peace with all his followers and how it is only through this divine peace that we could follow the commands to be at peace with our enemies and abusers.[2]

Whether ancient or modern, other scholars draw out different aspects of what peace is. Although peace can take different forms, here we start with the understanding that the peace God gives goes beyond our comprehension. There is a measure of peace that we can attain through human efforts; we can practice mindfulness-based stress reduction, go on a beach vacation, or cut back on our work hours. We can even try to make peace with a neighbor with whom we've argued in the past. Yet God's peace goes deeper than this because it is rooted in the work of God, the rightful Leader of the *basileia*, who came to his throne through Jesus Christ.

I recognize that it is a less daunting task for me to talk about making peace than it is for the people on the border of the US and Mexico. I have not had the deep history of abuse that too many others have experienced. I admit that my relative privilege influences my worldview, but I also see evidence of peace in the people of the Border Church. They seem to have a measure of peace despite the challenges they've faced. They've been abused. They've been vilified. They've been taken advantage of because of their language, race, gender, religion, and other aspects of their identities. Like Robert, though, when they come to the Border Church, peace fills their hearts. It's a *basileia* peace that makes some sense because they believe deeply in what is happening within the act of worship there under El Faro, but the peace goes deeper. That's because the Founder of the *basileia* is also the Giver of eternal peace.

Robert is someone who is trying to make peace in this world. His fierce work with and for migrants, alongside deported veterans, and within his own soul testifies to that. In his work, he seeks to put people on a better footing so that they have the best shot at thriving. Yet, Robert knows that his efforts are not always successful. He knows that sometimes you lose the fight. Glimpses of Christ's peace catch Robert's eye and the eyes of others along the borderlands. Feelings of *shalom* may not pervade these parts, but peaceful fruits are there along with seeds for future peace. Beneath it all is the root of Christ.

NOTES

1. John Chrysostom, "Homilies of St. John Chrysostom, Archbishop of Constantinople, on the Epistle of St. Paul the Apostle to the Philippians," in *Saint Chrysostom: Homilies on Galatians, Ephesians, Philippians, Colossians, Thessalonians, Timothy, Titus, and Philemon*, ed. Philip Schaff, trans. W. C. Cotton and John Albert Broadus, vol. 13, A Select Library of the Nicene and Post-Nicene Fathers of the Christian Church, First Series (New York: Christian Literature Company, 1889), 247.
2. Ibid.

EPILOGUE

The chapters in this book have each highlighted a mission or value of the Border Church with a story of one of its people. Throughout the chapters, we've explored following Jesus, the *basileia* of God, faith, hope, love, accompaniment, friendship, transformation, and peace. Although the chapters have come to a close, the real-life practices and actions that were illustrated throughout this book are far from over at Friendship Park. Here, where two nations meet by the sea, we will continue to seek unity in a place rife with division.

Our stories here will also continue to move forward. The *basileia* did not stop when the book was sent to the publisher or when your copy was printed or downloaded onto your device. Dreams of the borderlands looking a little more like heaven *do* come true. I write this filled with emotion as I can say that Robert has come home. On November 11, 2021, (yes, Veterans Day), Rober Vivar was let into the US as a free man. In a beautiful act of pastoral accompaniment, John Fanestil walked him across the borderline, and many of us welcomed Robert home. Welcome home, brother!

As for you, dear reader, I hope you can use what you learned from our little binational community of faith and apply it to your own spirituality, ministry, activism, or any other facet of life where these stories and concepts can help you promote the good across whatever boundaries exist in your own communities.

May God's *basileia* come, and may all our neighborhoods and churches—however many walls they have—look like they do in heaven. Amen.

SELECTED BIBLIOGRAPHY

Bird, Michael. *Evangelical Theology.* Grand Rapids, MI: Zondervan Academic, 2013.

Burridge, Andrew, Nick Gill, Austin Kocher, and Lauren Martin. "Polymorphic Borders." *Territory, Politics, Governance* 5, no. 3 (2017): 239–251.

Chrysostom, John. "Homilies of St. John Chrysostom, Archbishop of Constantinople, on the Epistle of St. Paul the Apostle to the Philippians." In *Saint Chrysostom: Homilies on Galatians, Ephesians, Philippians, Colossians, Thessalonians, Timothy, Titus, and Philemon.* Edited by Philip Schaff. Translated by W. C. Cotton and John Albert Broadus. Vol. 13. New York: Christian Literature Company, 1889.

Cruz, Gemma Tulud. *Toward a Theology of Migration.* New York: Palgrave Macmillan, 2014.

Hart, David Bentley. *That All Shall Be Saved: Heaven, Hell, and Universal Salvation.* New Haven, CT: Yale University Press, 2019.

Heimberger, Robert W. *God and the Illegal Alien: United States Immigration Law and a Theology of Politics.* Cambridge, UK: Cambridge University Press, 2018.

Jungkunz, Vincent. "The Promise of Democratic Silences." *New Political Science* 34, no. 2 (2012): 127–150.

Perrin, Nicholas. *The Kingdom of God.* Grand Rapids, MI: Zondervan Academic, 2019.

Prashad, Vijay. *The Karma of Brown Folk.* Minneapolis, MN: University of Minnesota Press, 2000.

Rohr, Richard. *Essential Teachings on Love.* Edited by Joelle Chase and Judy Traeger. Maryknoll, NY: Orbis Books, 2018.

Zaragoza, Barbara. *San Ysidro and the Tijuana River Valley.* Charlottesville, SC: Arcadia Publishing, 2014.